FIND HIM

BOOK OF MORMON
STUDY GUIDE

PERFECT FOR
COME, FOLLOW ME

BY GANEL-LYN CONDIE

& JOHN FOSSUM

Covenant
Communications, Inc.
www.covenant-lds.com

Cover image *Yea Lord* © Malory Fiso. For more information, go to www.foxandpebble.com.
Cover and interior design by Christina Marcano © 2023 by Covenant Communications, Inc.

Published by Covenant Communications, Inc.
American Fork, Utah

Printed in United States

First Printing: September 2023

30 29 28 27 26 25 24 23   10 9 8 7 6 5 4 3 1

ISBN 978-1-52442-511-1

PRAISE FOR *FIND HIM*

This little book is perfect to study with. I love that it's quick. It has a short commentary and quote about the study topic as well as a talking point and some space to write down your thoughts or aha's as you study.

—Amy

With so many resources out there, *Come, Follow Me* study can sometimes be overwhelming. What I love about John & Ganel-Lyn's . . . *Find Him* books is that they keep things short and sweet yet very meaningful and relatable.

—Brookelyn

I love this book. It's short and sweet and a perfect companion to the podcast.

—Kristi

I love the *Find Him* study guide. It is simple and helps you think for yourself. For so many years, I have searched for what others thought it was about rather than searching for myself. This is a very useful and soul-searching tool!

—Jennifer

Thank you for being genuine and sharing your human being-ness with us all. Thank you for sharing that it is about us coming unto Him. That act of going forward to let Heavenly Father and our Savior in, in order for them to help carry that heartache with us will heal us, comfort us, and strengthens our souls.

—Suny

The study guide *Find Him* is an excellent companion to . . . the *Come, Follow Me* program used by The Church of Jesus Christ of Latter-day Saints. I enjoy the comments of the authors and the prompts for journaling.

—LouRee

I love how easy it is to follow along and use this study guide with . . . the Church's *Come, Follow Me* lessons. It allows for the perfect amount of journaling room each week.

—Sutton

This is to help you record your own impressions while guiding you through *Come, Follow Me.* You can easily see a short overview and insights for the week, which scriptures to read, and then a space to record your own impressions. . . . It is short and sweet and meant to be a guide to stimulate your own thoughts and impressions.

—Stacie

This book is a simple guide that goes along with CFM each week. I like that it isn't adding tons of pages extra for me to have to read, but it's still insightful. . . . I'd recommend it if you just want a little extra to study each week.

—Dardie

365-DAY BOOK OF MORMON READING SCHEDULE

DAY #	DATE	SCRIPTURE BLOCK
1	Jan. 1	1 Nephi 1
2	Jan. 2	1 Nephi 2
3	Jan. 3	1 Nephi 3:1–14
4	Jan. 4	1 Nephi 3:15–31
5	Jan. 5	1 Nephi 4:1–18
6	Jan. 6	1 Nephi 4:19–38
7	Jan. 7	1 Nephi 5
8	Jan. 8	1 Nephi 6, 1 Nephi 7
9	Jan. 9	1 Nephi 8:1–19
10	Jan. 10	1 Nephi 8:20–38
11	Jan. 11	1 Nephi 9, 1 Nephi 10
12	Jan. 12	1 Nephi 11:1–20
13	Jan. 13	1 Nephi 11:21–36
14	Jan. 14	1 Nephi 12
15	Jan. 15	1 Nephi 13:1–11
16	Jan. 16	1 Nephi 13:12–29
17	Jan. 17	1 Nephi 13:30–42
18	Jan. 18	1 Nephi 14:1–15
19	Jan. 19	1 Nephi 14:16–30
20	Jan. 20	1 Nephi 15:1–20
21	Jan. 21	1 Nephi 15:21–36
22	Jan. 22	1 Nephi 16:1–20
23	Jan. 23	1 Nephi 16:21–39
24	Jan. 24	1 Nephi 17:1–18
25	Jan. 25	1 Nephi 17:19–35

DAY #	DATE	SCRIPTURE BLOCK
26	Jan. 26	1 Nephi 17:36–55
27	Jan. 27	1 Nephi 18:1–11
28	Jan. 28	1 Nephi 18: 12–25
29	Jan. 29	1 Nephi 19:1–10
30	Jan. 30	1 Nephi 19:11–24
31	Jan. 31	1 Nephi 20
32	Feb. 1	1 Nephi 21:1–13
33	Feb. 2	1 Nephi 21:14–26
34	Feb. 3	1 Nephi 22:1–14
35	Feb. 4	1 Nephi 22:15–31
36	Feb. 5	2 Nephi 1:1–16
37	Feb. 6	2 Nephi 1:17–32
38	Feb. 7	2 Nephi 2:1–16
39	Feb. 8	2 Nephi 2:17–30
40	Feb. 9	2 Nephi 3
41	Feb. 10	2 Nephi 4:1–18
42	Feb. 11	2 Nephi 4:19–35
43	Feb. 12	2 Nephi 5:1–17
44	Feb. 13	2 Nephi 5:18–34
45	Feb. 14	2 Nephi 6, 2 Nephi 7
46	Feb. 15	2 Nephi 8
47	Feb. 16	2 Nephi 9:1–18
48	Feb. 17	2 Nephi 9:19–36
49	Feb. 18	2 Nephi 9:37–54
50	Feb. 19	2 Nephi 10

DAY #	DATE	SCRIPTURE BLOCK
51	Feb. 20	2 Nephi 11
52	Feb. 21	2 Nephi 12
53	Feb. 22	2 Nephi 13
54	Feb. 23	2 Nephi 14, 2 Nephi 15
55	Feb. 24	2 Nephi 16, 2 Nephi 17
56	Feb. 25	2 Nephi 18
57	Feb. 26	2 Nephi 19
58	Feb. 27	2 Nephi 20
59	Feb. 28	2 Nephi 21, 2 Nephi 22
60	Mar. 1	2 Nephi 23
61	Mar. 2	2 Nephi 24:1–17
62	Mar. 3	2 Nephi 24:18–32
63	Mar. 4	2 Nephi 25:1–15
64	Mar. 5	2 Nephi 25:16–30
65	Mar. 6	2 Nephi 26
66	Mar. 7	2 Nephi 27:1–18
67	Mar. 8	2 Nephi 27:19–35
68	Mar. 9	2 Nephi 28:1–16
69	Mar. 10	2 Nephi 28:17–32
70	Mar. 11	2 Nephi 29
71	Mar. 12	2 Nephi 30
72	Mar. 13	2 Nephi 31
73	Mar. 14	2 Nephi 32
74	Mar. 15	2 Nephi 33
75	Mar. 16	Jacob 1
76	Mar. 17	Jacob 2:1–17
77	Mar. 18	Jacob 2:18–35
78	Mar. 19	Jacob 3

DAY #	DATE	SCRIPTURE BLOCK
79	Mar. 20	Jacob 4
80	Mar. 21	Jacob 5:1–16
81	Mar. 22	Jacob 5:17–32
82	Mar. 23	Jacob 5:33–48
83	Mar. 24	Jacob 5:49–64
84	Mar. 25	Jacob 5:65–77
85	Mar. 26	Jacob 6
86	Mar. 27	Jacob 7:1–13
87	Mar. 28	Jacob 7:14–27
88	Mar. 29	Enos 1
89	Mar. 30	Jarom 1
90	Mar. 31	Omni 1:1–14
91	April 1	Omni 1:15–30
92	April 2	Words of Mormon 1
93	April 3	Mosiah 1
94	April 4	Mosiah 2:1–13
95	April 5	Mosiah 2:14–27
96	April 6	Mosiah 2:28–41
97	April 7	Mosiah 3:1–13
98	April 8	Mosiah 3:14–27
99	April 9	Mosiah 4:1–15
100	April 10	Mosiah 4:16–30
101	April 11	Mosiah 5
102	April 12	Mosiah 6
103	April 13	Mosiah 7:1–16
104	April 14	Mosiah 7:17–33
105	April 15	Mosiah 8
106	April 16	Mosiah 9
107	April 17	Mosiah 10

DAY #	DATE	SCRIPTURE BLOCK
108	April 18	Mosiah 11:1–15
109	April 19	Mosiah 11:16–29
110	April 20	Mosiah 12:1–18
107	April 17	Mosiah 10
108	April 18	Mosiah 11:1–15
109	April 19	Mosiah 11:16–29
110	April 20	Mosiah 12:1–18
111	April 21	Mosiah 12:19–37
112	April 22	Mosiah 13:1–24
113	April 23	Mosiah 13:25–35, Mosiah 14
114	April 24	Mosiah 15
115	April 25	Mosiah 16
116	April 26	Mosiah 17
117	April 27	Mosiah 18:1–17
118	April 28	Mosiah 18:18–35
119	April 29	Mosiah 19
120	April 30	Mosiah 20
121	May 1	Mosiah 21:1–18
122	May 2	Mosiah 21:19–36
123	May 3	Mosiah 22
124	May 4	Mosiah 23:1–19
125	May 5	Mosiah 23:20–39
126	May 6	Mosiah 24
127	May 7	Mosiah 25
128	May 8	Mosiah 26:1–20
129	May 9	Mosiah 26:21–39
130	May 10	Mosiah 27:1–18
131	May 11	Mosiah 27:19–37
132	May 12	Mosiah 28

DAY #	DATE	SCRIPTURE BLOCK
133	May 13	Mosiah 29:1–15
134	May 14	Mosiah 29:16–30
135	May 15	Mosiah 29:31–47
136	May 16	Alma 1:1–18
137	May 17	Alma 1:19–33
138	May 18	Alma 2:1–19
139	May 19	Alma 2:20–38
140	May 20	Alma 3:1–12
141	May 21	Alma 3:13–27
142	May 22	Alma 4
143	May 23	Alma 5:1–21
144	May 24	Alma 5:22–42
145	May 25	Alma 5:43–62
146	May 26	Alma 6
147	May 27	Alma 7:1–14
148	May 28	Alma 7:15–27
149	May 29	Alma 8:1–17
150	May 30	Alma 8:18–32
151	May 31	Alma 9:1–17
152	June 1	Alma 9:18–34
153	June 2	Alma 10:1–14
154	June 3	Alma 10:15–32
155	June 4	Alma 11:1–22
156	June 5	Alma 11:23–46
157	June 6	Alma 12:1–19
158	June 7	Alma 12:20–37
159	June 8	Alma 13:1–16
160	June 9	Alma 13:17–31
161	June 10	Alma 14:1–16
162	June 11	Alma 14:17–29

DAY #	DATE	SCRIPTURE BLOCK
163	June 12	Alma 15
164	June 13	Alma 16:1–11
165	June 14	Alma 16:12–21
166	June 15	Alma 17:1–19
167	June 16	Alma 17:20–39
168	June 17	Alma 18:1–15
169	June 18	Alma 18:16–28
170	June 19	Alma 18:29–43
171	June 20	Alma 19:1–18
172	June 21	Alma 19:19–36
173	June 22	Alma 20:1–15
174	June 23	Alma 20:16–30
175	June 24	Alma 21
176	June 25	Alma 22:1–18
177	June 26	Alma 22:19–35
178	June 27	Alma 23
179	June 28	Alma 24:1–16
180	June 29	Alma 24:17–30
181	June 30	Alma 25
182	July 1	Alma 26:1–20
183	July 2	Alma 26:21–37
184	July 3	Alma 27:1–15
185	July 4	Alma 27:16–30
186	July 5	Alma 28
187	July 6	Alma 29
188	July 7	Alma 30:1–16
189	July 8	Alma 30:17–30
190	July 9	Alma 30:31–45
191	July 10	Alma 30:46–60
192	July 11	Alma 31:1–18

DAY #	DATE	SCRIPTURE BLOCK
193	July 12	Alma 31:19–38
194	July 13	Alma 32:1–15
195	July 14	Alma 32:16–29
196	July 15	Alma 32:30–43
197	July 16	Alma 33
198	July 17	Alma 34:1–21
199	July 18	Alma 34:22–41
200	July 19	Alma 35
201	July 20	Alma 36:1–15
202	July 21	Alma 36:16–30
203	July 22	Alma 37:1–15
204	July 23	Alma 37:16–31
205	July 24	Alma 37:32–47
206	July 25	Alma 38
207	July 26	Alma 39
208	July 27	Alma 40
209	July 28	Alma 41
210	July 29	Alma 42:1–16
211	July 30	Alma 42:17–31
212	July 31	Alma 43:1–18
213	Aug. 1	Alma 43:19–35
214	Aug. 2	Alma 43:36–54
215	Aug. 3	Alma 44:1–11
216	Aug. 4	Alma 44:12–24
217	Aug. 5	Alma 45
218	Aug. 6	Alma 46:1–21
219	Aug. 7	Alma 46:22–41
220	Aug. 8	Alma 47:1–18
221	Aug. 9	Alma 47:19–36
222	Aug. 10	Alma 48:1–13

DAY #	DATE	SCRIPTURE BLOCK	DAY #	DATE	SCRIPTURE BLOCK
223	Aug. 11	Alma 48:14–25	253	Sept. 10	Helaman 2
224	Aug. 12	Alma 49:1–15	254	Sept. 11	Helaman 3:1–18
225	Aug. 13	Alma 49:16–30	255	Sept. 12	Helaman 3:19–37
226	Aug. 14	Alma 50:1–21	256	Sept. 13	Helaman 4:1–13
227	Aug. 15	Alma 50:22–40	257	Sept. 14	Helaman 4:14–26
228	Aug. 16	Alma 51:1–21	258	Sept. 15	Helaman 5:1–16
229	Aug. 17	Alma 51:22–37	259	Sept. 16	Helaman 5:17–34
230	Aug. 18	Alma 52:1–20	260	Sept. 17	Helaman 5:35–52
231	Aug. 19	Alma 52:21–40	261	Sept. 18	Helaman 6:1–20
232	Aug. 20	Alma 53	262	Sept. 19	Helaman 6:21–41
233	Aug. 21	Alma 54	263	Sept. 20	Helaman 7:1–15
234	Aug. 22	Alma 55:1–17	264	Sept. 21	Helaman 7:16–29
235	Aug. 23	Alma 55:18–35	265	Sept. 22	Helaman 8
236	Aug. 24	Alma 56:1–20	266	Sept. 23	Helaman 9:1–20
237	Aug. 25	Alma 56:21–40	267	Sept. 24	Helaman 9:21–41
238	Aug. 26	Alma 56:41–57	268	Sept. 25	Helaman 10
239	Aug. 27	Alma 57:1–18	269	Sept. 26	Helaman 11:1–19
240	Aug. 28	Alma 57:19–36	270	Sept. 27	Helaman 11:20–38
241	Aug. 29	Alma 58:1–23	271	Sept. 28	Helaman 12:1–14
242	Aug. 30	Alma 58:24–41	272	Sept. 29	Helaman 12:15–26
243	Aug. 31	Alma 59	273	Sept. 30	Helaman 13:1–20
244	Sept. 1	Alma 60:1–19	274	Oct. 1	Helaman 13:21–39
245	Sept. 2	Alma 60:20–36	275	Oct. 2	Helaman 14:1–15
246	Sept. 3	Alma 61	276	Oct. 3	Helaman 14:16–31
247	Sept. 4	Alma 62:1–18	277	Oct. 4	Helaman 15
248	Sept. 5	Alma 62:19–36	278	Oct. 5	Helaman 16
249	Sept. 6	Alma 62:37–52	279	Oct. 6	3 Nephi 1:1–15
250	Sept. 7	Alma 62	280	Oct. 7	3 Nephi 1:16–30
251	Sept. 8	Helaman 1:1–17	281	Oct. 8	3 Nephi 2
252	Sept. 9	Helaman 1:18–34	282	Oct. 9	3 Nephi 3

DAY #	DATE	SCRIPTURE BLOCK
283	Oct. 10	3 Nephi 4:1–16
284	Oct. 11	3 Nephi 4:17–33
285	Oct. 12	3 Nephi 5:1–13
286	Oct. 13	3 Nephi 5:14–26
287	Oct. 14	3 Nephi 6:1–16
288	Oct. 15	3 Nephi 6:17–30
289	Oct. 16	3 Nephi 7:1–13
290	Oct. 17	3 Nephi 7:14–26
291	Oct. 18	3 Nephi 8
292	Oct. 19	3 Nephi 9
293	Oct. 20	3 Nephi 10
294	Oct. 21	3 Nephi 11:1–20
295	Oct. 22	3 Nephi 11:21–41
296	Oct. 23	3 Nephi 12:1–24
297	Oct. 24	3 Nephi 12:25–48
298	Oct. 25	3 Nephi 13:1–15
299	Oct. 26	3 Nephi 13:16–34
300	Oct. 27	3 Nephi 14
301	Oct. 28	3 Nephi 15
302	Oct. 29	3 Nephi 16
303	Oct. 30	3 Nephi 17
304	Oct. 31	3 Nephi 18:1–20
305	Nov. 1	3 Nephi 18:21–39
306	Nov. 2	3 Nephi 19:1–18
307	Nov. 3	3 Nephi 19:19–36
308	Nov. 4	3 Nephi 20:1–23
309	Nov. 5	3 Nephi 20:24–46
310	Nov. 6	3 Nephi 21
311	Nov. 7	3 Nephi 22
312	Nov. 8	3 Nephi 23

DAY #	DATE	SCRIPTURE BLOCK
313	Nov. 9	3 Nephi 24, 3 Nephi 25
314	Nov. 10	3 Nephi 26
315	Nov. 11	3 Nephi 27:1–17
316	Nov. 12	3 Nephi 27:18–33
317	Nov. 13	3 Nephi 28:1–23
318	Nov. 14	3 Nephi 28:24–40
319	Nov. 15	3 Nephi 29, 3 Nephi 30
320	Nov. 16	4 Nephi 1:1–26
321	Nov. 17	4 Nephi 1:27–49
322	Nov. 18	Mormon 1
323	Nov. 19	Mormon 2:1–15
324	Nov. 20	Mormon 2:16–29
325	Nov. 21	Mormon 3
326	Nov. 22	Mormon 4
327	Nov. 23	Mormon 5:1–11
328	Nov. 24	Mormon 5:12–24
329	Nov. 25	Mormon 6
330	Nov. 26	Mormon 7
331	Nov. 27	Mormon 8:1–21
332	Nov. 28	Mormon 8:22–41
333	Nov. 29	Mormon 9:1–20
334	Nov. 30	Mormon 9:21–37
335	Dec. 1	Ether 1:1–32
336	Dec. 2	Ether 1:33–43
337	Dec. 3	Ether 2
338	Dec. 4	Ether 3:1–13
339	Dec. 5	Ether 3:14–28
340	Dec. 6	Ether 4
341	Dec. 7	Ether 5

DAY #	DATE	SCRIPTURE BLOCK
342	Dec. 8	Ether 6:1–15
343	Dec. 9	Ether 6:16–30
344	Dec. 10	Ether 7
345	Dec. 11	Ether 8
346	Dec. 12	Ether 9:1–19
347	Dec. 13	Ether 9:20–35
348	Dec. 14	Ether 10:1–18
349	Dec. 15	Ether 10:19–34
350	Dec. 16	Ether 11
351	Dec. 17	Ether 12:1–22
352	Dec. 18	Ether 12:23–41
353	Dec. 19	Ether 13:1–15
354	Dec. 20	Ether 13:16–31
355	Dec. 21	Ether 14
356	Dec. 22	Ether 15:1–17
357	Dec. 23	Ether 15:18–34
358	Dec. 24	Moroni 1, Moroni 2, Moroni 3
359	Dec. 25	Moroni 4, Moroni 5, Moroni 6
360	Dec. 26	Moroni 7:1–24
361	Dec. 27	Moroni 7:25–48
362	Dec. 28	Moroni 8
363	Dec. 29	Moroni 9
364	Dec. 30	Moroni 10:1–17
365	Dec. 31	Moroni 10:18–34

CFM: BOM STUDY SCHEDULE

Jan 1–7: Introductory Pages of the Book of Mormon—Another Testament of Jesus Christ

Jan 8–14: 1 Nephi 1–5—"I Will Go and Do"

Jan 15–21: 1 Nephi 6–10—"Come and Partake of the Fruit"

Jan 22–28: 1 Nephi 11–15—"Armed with Righteousness and with the Power of God"

Jan 29–Feb 4: 1 Nephi 16–22—"I Will Prepare the Way before You"

Feb 5–11: 2 Nephi 1–2—"Free to Choose Liberty and Eternal Life, through the Great Mediator"

Feb 12–18: 2 Nephi 3–5—"We Lived after the Manner of Happiness"

Feb 19–25: 2 Nephi 6–10—"O How Great the Plan of Our God"

Feb 26–Mar 3: 2 Nephi 11–19—"His Name Shall Be Called . . . the Prince of Peace"

Mar 4–10: 2 Nephi 20–25—"We Rejoice in Christ"

Mar 11–17: 2 Nephi 26–30—"A Marvelous Work and a Wonder"

Mar 18–24: 2 Nephi 31–33—"This Is the Way"

Mar 25–31: Easter—"He Shall Rise . . . with Healing in His Wings"

Apr 1–7: Jacob 1–4—Be Reconciled unto God through the Atonement of Christ

Apr 8–14: Jacob 5–7—The Lord Labors with Us

Apr 15–21: Enos–Words of Mormon—"He Worketh in Me to Do According to His Will"

Apr 22–28: Mosiah 1–3—"Filled with Love Towards God and All Men"

Apr 29–May 5: Mosiah 4–6—"A Mighty Change"

May 6–12: Mosiah 7–10—"In the Strength of the Lord"

May 13–19: Mosiah 11–17—"A Light . . . That Can Never Be Darkened"

May 20–26: Mosiah 18–24—We Have Entered into a Covenant with Him

May 27–Jun 2: Mosiah 25–28—"They Were Called the People of God"

Jun 3–9: Mosiah 29–Alma 4—"They Were Steadfast and Immovable"

Jun 10–16: Alma 5–7—"Have Ye Experienced This Mighty Change in Your Hearts?"

INTRODUCTION TO THE FIND HIM: BOOK OF MORMON STUDY GUIDE

Mormon 5:14

> *And behold, [the Book of Mormon] shall go unto the unbelieving of the Jews; and for this intent shall [it] go—that they may be persuaded that Jesus is the Christ, the Son of the living God; that the Father may bring about, through his most Beloved, his great and eternal purpose, in restoring the Jews, or all the house of Israel, to the land of their inheritance, which the Lord their God hath given them, unto the fulfilling of his covenant.*

D&C 33:16

> *And the Book of Mormon and the holy scriptures are given of me for your instruction; and the power of my Spirit quickeneth all things.*

We can't wait to study the Book of Mormon with you this year and collectively recommit ourselves to make this inspired book of scripture a central component of our worship! With the Spirit as our guide, we will discover Jesus Christ on every page, and God's light will grow within each of us.

The Book of Mormon was brought forth by God through Joseph Smith to serve as another testament of the divine Sonship of Jesus Christ. Since its official publication in 1829, millions of people have experienced a greater connection with God and clarity in their understanding of the purpose of Jesus Christ and His atoning sacrifice. We feel confident that this Book of Mormon study guide will help you experience and strengthen your own heavenly witness of the reality of the Savior of the world and His holy purpose to save and exalt all humankind.

Mormon, the ancient prophet after whom the Book of Mormon is named, explained the purpose of this additional scriptural record. He said that the Book of Mormon would come forth in the latter days so that those who do *not* believe in Jesus "may be persuaded that Jesus is the Christ, the Son of the living God; that the Father may bring about, through his most Beloved, his great and eternal purpose, . . . unto the fulfilling of his covenant" (Mormon 5:14). It is our testimony that if you read and study the Book of Mormon "with a sincere heart, with real intent, having faith in Christ, [God] will manifest the truth of it unto you, by the power of the Holy Ghost" (Moroni 10:4).

In 2018, The Church of Jesus Christ of Latter-day Saints introduced "an integrated curriculum to strengthen families and individuals through a *home-centered* and *Church-supported* plan to learn doctrine, strengthen faith, and foster greater personal worship" (Russell M. Nelson, "Opening Remarks," *Ensign* or *Liahona*, November 2018). As part of this inspired initiative, the *Come, Follow Me* (CFM) scripture study program was presented. The CFM approach to personal scripture study elevates the role of personal insights and Spirit-driven revelations, specifically emphasizing that "we are each responsible for our individual spiritual growth" (Russell M. Nelson, "Opening Remarks").

With these inspired prophetic goals in mind, this study guide, *Find Him*, was written. Our intent has always been, and will continue to be, to help motivate individuals to dive into the scriptures, trust the tutelage of the Spirit, and become more spiritually self-reliant as they are taught from heaven. These goals are especially important when we consider God's warning to members of the Church back in 1832 for not using the Book of Mormon to its fullest extent. He said that members of the Church would experience a type of spiritual condemnation "until they repent and remember the new covenant, even the Book of Mormon and the former commandments which I have given them, not only to say, but to do according to that which I have written" (D&C 84:57).

As President Russell M. Nelson taught, "Few things build faith more than does regular immersion in the Book of Mormon. No other book testifies of Jesus Christ with such power and clarity. Its prophets, as inspired by the Lord, saw our day and selected the doctrine and truths that would help *us* most. The Book of Mormon *is* our *latter-day* survival guide" ("Embrace the Future with Faith," *Ensign* or *Liahona*, November 2020).

We named this study guide *Find Him* because it is intended to assist you in your personal journey to discover Jesus. It can be used independently with any other resource you may find helpful!

It includes scripture passages, personal and prophetic insights, and questions and prompts to foster more discovery. However you choose to use this study guide, we hope it helps you find Him more in your life each week.

President Nelson said, "Through personal revelation, you can receive your own witness that the Book of Mormon is the word of God. . . . Regardless of what others may say or do, no one can ever take away a witness borne to your heart and mind about what is true" ("Revelation for the Church, Revelation for Our Lives," *Ensign* or *Liahona*, May 2018). It is our hope and prayer that *Find Him*, combined with other study resources, will help you acquire and strengthen your own personal witness of Jesus Christ.

JAN 1–JAN 7: ANOTHER TESTAMENT OF JESUS CHRIST

INTRODUCTORY PAGES OF THE BOM

Title Page
Paragraph 2

> *[The Book of Mormon is meant] to show unto the remnant of the house of Israel what great things the Lord hath done for their fathers; and that they may know the covenants of the Lord, that they are not cast off forever—And also to the convincing of the Jew and Gentile that JESUS is the CHRIST, the ETERNAL GOD, manifesting himself unto all nations.*

The title page of the Book of Mormon was written by the ancient prophet Moroni, and it provides the central thesis for the entire book. According to Moroni, if we read the Book of Mormon in the same spirit it was written, "the spirit of prophecy and revelation," then we will acquire a testimony of three specific things:

1. We will realize and appreciate all the "great things the Lord hath done" for His children in the past,

2. We will learn "the covenants of the Lord" and discover that none of God's children are "cast off forever," and

3. We will know that "JESUS is the CHRIST, the ETERNAL GOD," and that all of the beautiful realities of God's plan are made possible through Him.

If we study the Book of Mormon and don't come away with more faith and optimism in the salvific outcomes of God's plan, then we have missed the point. On every page of the Book of Mormon, the Spirit can help us see one or more of the three purposes given to us by Moroni. The Book of Mormon offers "joy and hidden treasures" to all who will read it with faith in Jesus Christ (Russell M. Nelson, "'Come, Follow Me,'" *Ensign* or *Liahona*, May 2019).

TALKING POINT

Most of the original witnesses of the Book of Mormon fell away from the Church despite having "seen the plates" and testifying that the Book of Mormon had become "marvelous in [their] eyes" ("The Testimony of Three Witnesses").

What is the difference between something becoming "marvelous in our eyes" and it becoming marvelous in our hearts?

And what will you do to make sure the Book of Mormon becomes marvelous in your heart?

JAN 8–JAN 14: "I WILL GO AND DO"

1 NEPHI 1–5

1 Nephi 3:7, 31

And it came to pass that I, Nephi, said unto my father: I will go and do the things which the Lord hath commanded, for I know that the Lord giveth no commandments unto the children of men, save he shall prepare a way for them that they may accomplish the thing which he commandeth them.

And after the angel had departed, Laman and Lemuel again began to murmur, saying: How is it possible that the Lord will deliver Laban into our hands? Behold, he is a mighty man, and he can command fifty, yea, even he can slay fifty; then why not us?

One of the most quoted verses of the Book of Mormon is found in 1 Nephi 3:7. It speaks of a faith so strong it can move mountains and a trust in God that opens the way to accomplish even the impossible. Nephi's example of trust and obedience is awe-inspiring. What would it take for us to be so faithful?

Perhaps if we could talk face-to-face with an angel, then we really could "do the things which the Lord hath commanded." But as we read about Laman and Lemuel in 1 Nephi 3:31, seeing an angel doesn't guarantee a willing and obedient heart. Rather than trusting, they doubted, saying, "How is it possible that the Lord will deliver Laban into our hands?"

As we read more of Nephi's faith journey, we see that each experience he has strengthens his resolve

TALKING POINT

We often see the hand of God when looking back at a situation we've experienced. Share with your family or a friend a time when you felt God asking you to do something that scared you. How did responding to the command strengthen your faith? How did God prepare the way?

to follow God's commands, while his brothers fear even as they stand in front of heavenly messengers.

Elder Larry S. Kacher said,

> Unbelief blocks our ability to see miracles, whereas a mindset of faith in the Savior unlocks the powers of heaven. Even when our faith is weak, the Lord's hand will always be stretched out. ("Ladder of Faith," *Liahona*, May 2022)

I don't think the Book of Mormon points to a Nephi who lived in a constant state of faith and zero fear, but I do think it shows us that he worked on consistently strengthening his faith muscle, much like a dedicated athlete works on their body. Choosing faith and trust in God when our circumstances point us toward fear is when our faith grows and deepens.

JAN 15–21: "COME AND PARTAKE OF THE FRUIT"

1 NEPHI 6–10

1 Nephi 8:10, 12

And it came to pass that I beheld a tree, whose fruit was desirable to make one happy.

And as I partook of the fruit thereof it filled my soul with exceedingly great joy . . .

Do the life and teachings of Jesus influence all your thoughts and words each day? Lehi saw in vision just how central Jesus Christ is to God's plan of happiness. Consider how impossible it would be for us to successfully navigate life's "dark and dreary wilderness" (1 Nephi 8:4) without "a rod of iron" (verse 19) to cleave to and "a straight and narrow path" (verse 20) to follow.

Both the rod of iron and the path are symbols of Jesus Christ. Additionally, both the tree Lehi saw and its fruit, which was "desirable to make one happy" (1 Nephi 8:10), are direct symbols of God's love, encompassed in the atoning sacrifice and grace of Jesus Christ. Lehi's vision makes it clear that if we want to successfully make our way through the "dark and dreary waste" (verse 7) we encounter in life and partake of the sweet fruit of the tree of life, our daily focus has to be on Jesus. Lehi's vision helps us "realize that without Jesus Christ, we are doomed, but with Him, we can receive the greatest gift Heavenly Father can give" (Dale G. Renlund, "Consider the Goodness and Greatness of God," *Ensign* or *Liahona*, May 2020).

TALKING POINT

This week, consider studying 1 Nephi 8 in conjunction with Elder David A. Bednar's talk "But We Heeded Them Not." Record your Spirit-driven thoughts and impressions about how you can make Jesus Christ more central in your daily life.

JAN 22–28: "ARMED WITH RIGHTEOUSNESS AND WITH THE POWER OF GOD"

1 NEPHI 11–15

1 Nephi 11:25

> *And it came to pass that I beheld that the rod of iron, which my father had seen, was the word of God, which led to the fountain of living waters, or to the tree of life; which waters are a representation of the love of God; and I also beheld that the tree of life was a representation of the love of God.*

Imagine you just fell in love with a new ice cream flavor at first taste. It is so good you want to share it with the world. You call your friend and tell her about it. You even find a discount coupon code for the ice cream shop and text it to her so she has no excuse not to run down to get her own cone.

A few weeks later, you are talking with your friend, and you ask how she likes the ice cream. She admits that she hasn't tried it yet. How do you feel?

To compare the love of God to ice cream is obviously lacking in eternal intensity and importance. But I hope the analogy helps illustrate what it feels like to experience His love.

Lehi wanted to share the experience of tasting God's love with his family. He invited, encouraged, and pleaded to have them partake of the fruit he had tasted.

The love of God has the power to sanctify and save. No ice cream I know of has that kind of impact. Yet why is it easier to share a restaurant recommendation than a scripture insight?

Elder Neal A. Maxwell taught,

> Laman and Lemuel became rebels instead of leaders, resentful instead of righteous—all because of their failure to understand either the character or the purposes of God. . . .

. . . True, we could know more facts about them, but it would not change the "bottom line." If, in some respects, they seem to be undeveloped characters, it is because theirs was a haunting emptiness, which could have been filled by the "love of God." In vision, . . . Lehi saw them, "but they would not . . . partake of the fruit" (1 Ne. 8:17–18; see also 1 Ne. 11:25; 1 Ne. 8:35; 2 Ne. 5:20). Of all self-inflicted punishments, this eight-word epitaph describes the most awful and consequential! ("Lessons from Laman and Lemuel," *Ensign* or *Liahona*, November 1999)

Once we taste the love of God, it changes everything. When you truly understand the nature of God, it gives hope for healing and strength in the Savior.

TALKING POINT

Once we taste the love of God, it is easy to understand why we would want to invite others to partake. Is there a scripture verse, a worship song, or a piece of art that helps you feel God's love? Consider sharing this with someone who may not have tasted the fruit of God's love for a while.

JAN 29–FEB 4: "I WILL PREPARE THE WAY BEFORE YOU"

1 NEPHI 16–22

1 Nephi 21:25

But thus saith the Lord, even the captives of the mighty shall be taken away, and the prey of the terrible shall be delivered; for I will contend with him that contendeth with thee, and I will save thy children.

We often stress about loved ones who are spiritually lost. The prophet Nephi used the writings of Isaiah to specifically "persuade [us] to believe in the Lord [our] Redeemer" (1 Nephi 19:23). Nephi knew that if our testimony of Jesus Christ and His mission was strengthened, we would be filled with hope for *all* of God's children, but especially for those who "have been broken off" (verse 24).

> **TALKING POINT**
>
> Study 1 Nephi 20–22 while thinking of one or more people from your life who have strayed from the covenant path. What promises and realities do Isaiah and Nephi emphasize that can give you hope for these individuals?

God promised through Isaiah that "thy children shall make haste against thy destroyers" (1 Nephi 21:17), and "even the captives of the mighty shall be taken away, and the prey of the terrible shall be delivered" (verse 25). Then He said, "For I will contend with him that contendeth with thee, and I will save thy children" (verse 25).

The experiences of Lehi and his family in the wilderness illustrate that God will lead us through our personal deserts "in an acceptable time" (1 Nephi 21:8). And as Isaiah testified, God will also "bring [us] again out of captivity, and . . . [we] shall be brought out of obscurity and out of darkness; and [we] shall know that the Lord is [our] Savior and [our] Redeemer, the Mighty One of Israel" (1 Nephi 22:12).

FEB 5–11: "FREE TO CHOOSE LIBERTY AND ETERNAL LIFE, THROUGH THE GREAT MEDIATOR"

2 NEPHI 1–2

2 Nephi 2:27

Wherefore, men are free according to the flesh; and all things are given them which are expedient unto man. And they are free to choose liberty and eternal life, through the great Mediator of all men, or to choose captivity and death, according to the captivity and power of the devil; for he seeketh that all men might be miserable like unto himself.

Agency is the gift that opens the door for more gifts. When we choose God, He gives the gifts of liberty and freedom. Alternately, when we choose the adversary, he gives captivity and pain.

Elder Jörg Klebingat taught, "God *won't* force us to do good, and the devil *can't* force us to do evil. Though some may think that mortality is a contest between God and the adversary, a word from the Savior 'and Satan is silenced and banished. . . . It is [our] strength that is being tested—not God's'" ("Valiant Discipleship in the Latter Days," *Liahona*, May 2022).

I loved reading pick-your-own-ending books as a child. It was fun to see how choosing one way got you to a certain place. However, life is not like these books. We are each given this one mortal mission with no going back and picking different endings. Yet we have the power to choose the right each day as we repent and strive to follow the Savior.

TALKING POINT

For home evening this week, play a pick-your-own-ending game with some hypothetical choices. Have a discussion with friends or family about the greater liberty versus captivity players experienced based on the decisions they made.

FEB 12–18: "WE LIVED AFTER THE MANNER OF HAPPINESS"

2 NEPHI 3–5

2 Nephi 4:20–21

My God hath been my support; he hath led me through mine afflictions in the wilderness; and he hath preserved me upon the waters of the great deep.

He hath filled me with his love, even unto the consuming of my flesh.

I sometimes struggle with feeling like I am not enough, and I think Nephi had similar feelings. In 2 Nephi 4, Nephi lamented, "O wretched man that I am!" (verse 17). But after a brief spiritual wrestle, Nephi emerged comforted and content with his efforts to become like God. He had been relying too much on his own efforts and needed to trust God's love and the merits of Jesus Christ.

President Dieter F. Uchtdorf said,

> I learned in my life that we don't need to be "more" of anything to start to become the person God intended us to become.
>
> God will take you as you are at this very moment and begin to work with you. All you need is a willing heart, a desire to believe, and trust in the Lord. ("It Works Wonderfully!," *Ensign* or *Liahona*, November 2015)

Do you *want* to be better today than you were yesterday? Are you *willing* to try to become more like Jesus? If so, then God is pleased with your efforts and will continue to bless you with the grace you need to learn and grow. Be patient with yourself, and remember that anyone who chooses to yoke themselves with Jesus is enough, because Jesus is *more* than enough!

TALKING POINT

As you study the Psalm of Nephi this week (2 Nephi 4), also read and ponder similar truths taught by Elder Dieter F. Uchtdorf in his talk "The Hope of God's Light." Record the impressions given to you by the Spirit about God's love and your divine potential.

FEB 19–25: "O HOW GREAT THE PLAN OF OUR GOD"

2 NEPHI 6–10

2 Nephi 9:21

And he cometh into the world that he may save all men if they will hearken unto his voice; for behold, he suffereth the pains of all men, yea, the pains of every living creature, both men, women, and children, who belong to the family of Adam.

Jesus came to save and succor. He came to suffer so we don't have to suffer alone and eternally. But knowing Christ is there and that He understands us may not always feel like it is enough to sustain us spiritually and emotionally. Special awareness and care may need to be considered for those wrestling with specific pains.

For those who experience the stewardship of mental illness, the suffering can be exhausting and chronic. Those within faith communities can and should lead the way in normalizing conversations about these overwhelming issues. We should be at the forefront of creating safe spaces for those who wrestle with both the episodic and ongoing challenges associated with a variety of neurological differences.

Elder Erich W. Kopischke said, "Because mental illness can interfere with our perception of perfection, it remains all too often a taboo. As a result, there is too much ignorance, too much silent suffering, and too much despair. Many, feeling overwhelmed because they do not meet perceived standards, mistakenly believe they have no place in the Church" ("Addressing Mental Health," *Liahona*, November 2021).

The Savior knows our individual needs, pains, and struggles. Because He took upon Himself all of our pains, Jesus knows how to succor us. The Savior knows how to heal the broken and comfort the exhausted.

My own family has endured many mental health challenges, including depression, anxiety, ADD, and even suicidal loss and grief. But through it all, we have felt God meet us where we were and give us His power to carry on. He has promised to save all of us if we continue to hearken to His voice. Don't give up. We will never be better without you.

TALKING POINT

Have a dinner conversation this week about mental health. Ask for a check-in from everyone in your home, having them rank their mental health status on a scale from one to ten. Consider sharing on social media or with a friend one resource—such as therapy, meditation, or daily movement—that has helped you with your mental health.

FEB 26–MAR 3: "HIS NAME SHALL BE CALLED . . . THE PRINCE OF PEACE"

2 NEPHI 11–19

2 Nephi 12:3–4

> *And many people shall go and say, Come ye, and let us go up to the mountain of the Lord, to the house of the God of Jacob; and he will teach us of his ways, and we will walk in his paths. . . .*
>
> *And he shall judge among the nations, and shall rebuke many people: and they shall beat their swords into plow-shares, and their spears into pruning-hooks—nation shall not lift up sword against nation, neither shall they learn war any more.*

The prophet Nephi announced his reason for quoting Isaiah: "Whoso . . . shall see these words may lift up their hearts and rejoice for all men" (2 Nephi 11:8). Isaiah's message is one of hope for anyone who is spiritually struggling or who may find themselves currently captive to darkness. After reading Isaiah, we should feel *more* confident in the future exaltation of God's children.

Isaiah's writings follow what I refer to as the Hope Cycle. He:

1. Candidly calls out our wickedness,

2. Explains what will happen if our current course doesn't change, then

3. Finishes with some of the most hope-filled promises in all of scripture.

For example, despite Israel's consistent rebellious backslidings, God promised that someday "he will lift up an *ensign* to the nations from far" and redeem His children (2 Nephi 15:26).

Wherever there is hope and healing, you will find Jesus. Prophesying of the future Savior, Isaiah saw a day when "people that walked in darkness [would see] a great light," and "they that dwell in the

TALKING POINT

As you read through the Isaiah chapters of 2 Nephi, look for how many times you can identify the Hope Cycle. It may help to write "Hope" next to any power phrase or verse that points to a future day of healing and joy for those who are spiritually struggling or lost.

land of the shadow of death, upon them [will] the light shine" (2 Nephi 19:2). There is no amount of darkness that Jesus Christ cannot dispel. That is why we refer to Him as "Wonderful, Counselor, The Mighty God, The Everlasting Father, The Prince of Peace" (verse 6).

MAR 4–10: "WE REJOICE IN CHRIST"

2 NEPHI 20–25

2 Nephi 25:26

And we talk of Christ, we rejoice in Christ, we preach of Christ, we prophesy of Christ, and we write according to our prophecies, that our children may know to what source they may look for a remission of their sins.

"The most powerful spiritual influence in the life of a child is the righteous example of loving parents and grandparents who faithfully keep their own sacred covenants" (Kevin W. Pearson, "Are You Still Willing?," *Liahona*, November 2022).

While raising my children, I tried to find natural ways to speak of Christ. When they came home from school or as we ate dinner together, instead of asking, "How was your day?" I would often ask, "What mistake did you make today?" They would hesitantly review their day and share a mistake made, assignment missed, or unkind word spoken. After my children confessed their transgressions, I would cheer and celebrate. It may seem odd, but I was trying to teach an important principle—mistakes are how we learn. Normalizing mistakes for my kids opened up conversations about mercy, grace, repentance, and making amends.

Elder Neil L. Andersen said, "As the world speaks less of Jesus Christ, let us speak more of Him. . . . As we share the light we have received from Him, His light and His transcendent saving power will shine on those willing to open their hearts. Jesus said, 'I . . . come [as] a light into the world.'" ("We Talk of Christ," *Ensign* or *Liahona*, November 2020).

TALKING POINT

This week, plan a daily celebration of the mistakes you make.
How does taking the time to celebrate your mistakes help you rejoice in Christ and His Atonement more?

We can rejoice in daily repentance. We can talk of how Christ has helped us with our mistakes so that our children know to what source they too can turn for help.

MAR 11–17: "A MARVELOUS WORK AND A WONDER"

2 NEPHI 26–30

2 Nephi 28:29

Wo be unto him that shall say: We have received the word of God, and we need no more of the word of God, for we have enough!

Our ninth article of faith states, "We believe . . . that [God] will yet reveal many great and important things pertaining to the Kingdom of God." I love the thought that "many great and important things" are *yet* to be revealed. As beautiful as the Restoration has been since 1820, some of the best gems of the Restoration are *yet* to come! President Russell M. Nelson said, "We're witnesses to a process of restoration. . . . If you think the Church has been fully restored, you're just seeing the beginning. There is much more to come. . . . It's going to be exciting" (in "Latter-day Saint Prophet, Wife and Apostle Share Insights of Global Ministry," https://newsroom.churchofjesuschrist.org/article/latter-day-saint-prophet-wife-apostle-share-insights-global-ministry).

Believe it or not, some people are not excited about the reality of what the prophet and apostles refer to as "the ongoing Restoration." Much of people's perceived spiritual stability comes from their hasty belief that we have *already* received a fullness of what God has to offer and that our responsibility is simply to tell others about it. However, our modern-day prophet and apostles are actively prepping us for much more to come!

Nephi saw a vision of latter-day earth full of people who will *not* want more light. Many will simply be distracted (see 2 Nephi 28:5–20), but others will assume that they already know everything (see verses 21–30). Both groups are equally unable to receive further light and knowledge. God said through Nephi, "For unto him that receiveth I will give more; and from them that shall say, We have enough, from them shall be taken away" (verse 30). If we want to receive the blessings of the ongoing Restoration, then we must reassess everything we think we know and look forward to the "many great and important things" to come. President Nelson put it this way: "The ongoing Restoration needs ongoing revelation" ("The Temple and Your Spiritual Foundation," *Liahona*, November 2021).

TALKING POINT

Make a list of all the aspects of the gospel and our worship that God has clarified or added to since Russell M. Nelson became the prophet in 2018. While studying 2 Nephi 26–30 this week, consider what you can do to ensure you stay in-stride with the ongoing Restoration.

MAR 18–24: "THIS IS THE WAY"

2 NEPHI 31–33

2 Nephi 31:20

Wherefore, ye must press forward with a steadfastness in Christ, having a perfect brightness of hope, and a love of God and of all men. Wherefore, if ye shall press forward, feasting upon the word of Christ, and endure to the end, behold, thus saith the Father: Ye shall have eternal life.

I have a friend who has never married. She wants to be married and has petitioned heaven for help. I have learned a lot from her about having a perfect brightness of hope and pressing forward with a steadfastness in Christ. She taught me how easily we may focus on what we *don't have* instead of seeing all that we do have by sharing an insight about Adam and Eve. They had a garden full of trees to choose from but seemed overly distracted by the one tree they had been commanded not to partake of.

This kind of tunnel vision can easily happen in all of our lives. Worries about children, financial burdens, unmet dreams, or chronic illness can easily become our focus. The lack, instead of the abundance, is the one tree we see—and not the lush forest of blessings around us.

TALKING POINT

Try to focus on the forest of trees (blessings) God has given you. Identify a scripture verse that helps you stay hopeful, then each day this week, write down five things you are grateful for.

But how do we appreciate all we have instead of only seeing all we don't? 2 Nephi 31:20 gives the answer: Feast upon the word of Christ, press forward in faith, endure to the end with hope and love of God, and we will have eternal life—which means everything.

MAR 25–31: "HE SHALL RISE . . . WITH HEALING IN HIS WINGS"

EASTER

2 Nephi 2:8

> *Wherefore, how great the importance to make these things known unto the inhabitants of the earth, that they may know that there is no flesh that can dwell in the presence of God, save it be through the merits, and mercy, and grace of the Holy Messiah, who layeth down his life according to the flesh, and taketh it again by the power of the Spirit, that he may bring to pass the resurrection of the dead, being the first that should rise.*

2 Nephi 10:25

> *Wherefore, may God raise you from death by the power of the resurrection, and also from everlasting death by the power of the atonement, that ye may be received into the eternal kingdom of God, that ye may praise him through grace divine. Amen.*

Without the Resurrection of Jesus Christ on that first Easter morning, there would be no plan of redemption to speak of, and all of our cherished beliefs and faith practices would become meaningless. Thankfully, Jesus *did* rise from the grave and "shewed himself alive . . . by many infallible proofs" (Acts 1:3). His emergence from the tomb signaled the completion of His atoning sacrifice and guaranteed our eternal access to God's grace, healing, and power.

Elder Jeffrey R. Holland once referred to Easter as "the most sacred day of the year for special remembrance of brotherly hands and determined arms that reached into the abyss of death to save us from our fallings and our failings, from our sorrows and our sins" ("Where Justice, Love, and Mercy Meet," *Ensign* or *Liahona*, May 2015). As we sing in the famous Easter hymn celebrating Jesus's Resurrection,

Death is conquered; man is free.

Christ has won the victory.

("He Is Risen!" *Hymns*, no. 199)

This Easter, let us celebrate and give thanks for Jesus Christ's universal victory over sin and death, which opened heaven's gate for all of God's children to return to Him. Elder Gerrit W. Gong said, "[Jesus Christ] came and comes to heal the brokenhearted, deliver the captives, recover sight to the blind, and set at liberty those who are bruised. That's each of us. His redeeming promises apply, no matter our past, our present, or concerns for our future" ("Hosanna and Hallelujah—The Living Jesus Christ: The Heart of Restoration and Easter," *Ensign* or *Liahona*, May 2020).

TALKING POINT

On Easter Sunday, start a conversation with a family member or friend about what they most look forward to in the future Resurrection. How can focusing on those future realities help you endure the burdens you currently bear?

Supplemental Easter Week Study Help

Scan the QR code to study the events of each day of the week leading up to Jesus's Resurrection.

APR 1–7: BE RECONCILED UNTO GOD THROUGH THE ATONEMENT OF CHRIST

JACOB 1–4

Jacob 4:13

> *Behold, my brethren, he that prophesieth, let him prophesy to the understanding of men; for the Spirit speaketh the truth and lieth not. Wherefore, it speaketh of things as they really are, and of things as they really will be; wherefore, these things are manifested unto us plainly, for the salvation of our souls. But behold, we are not witnesses alone in these things; for God also spake them unto prophets of old.*

A few years ago, it became obvious that I needed glasses. I not only needed help seeing far away but also reading anything smaller than an eighteen-point font. After a trip to the eye doctor, I got a pair of bifocals. It was amazing to see again. My scripture reading was easier. When watching a movie or attending church, I noticed what I hadn't noticed. The truth was I thought I was seeing clearly, but clearly I wasn't.

Sister Tracy Y. Browning taught some of the many ways the Lord helps us see clearly in our lives: "Our Savior, Jesus Christ, directs our feet to meetinghouses each week to partake of His sacrament, to the house of the Lord to make covenants with Him, to the scriptures and teachings of prophets to learn of His words. He directs our mouths to testify of Him, our hands to lift and serve as He would lift and serve, our eyes to see the world and each other as He does— 'as they really are, and . . . as they really will be'" ("Seeing More of Jesus Christ in Our Lives," *Liahona*, November 2022).

How often are we walking through life not seeing people clearly? Our vision is blurred by biases and beliefs. But with the Spirit, we can see others as they really are and how God sees them.

Our wards, homes, and neighborhoods will change as we begin to see one another as we really are—divine siblings and children of God.

TALKING POINT

Choose one person who may have triggered you or even offended you in the past. For the next seven days, pray to see them as God does. At the end of the week, consider sending this person a note or text acknowledging the divine qualities you appreciate about them.

APR 8–14: THE LORD LABORS WITH US

JACOB 5–7

Jacob 5:41, 61

And it came to pass that the Lord of the vineyard wept, and said unto the servant: What could I have done more for my vineyard?

Wherefore, go to, and call servants, that we may labor diligently with our might in the vineyard, that we may prepare the way, that I may bring forth again the natural fruit, which natural fruit is good and the most precious above all other fruit.

An arborist is someone who cares for trees. One of my favorite definitions for *arborist* is "tree surgeon." Regular care for trees involves lots of pruning and watering and fertilizing. Jacob 5 helps us understand why God is the Master Arborist!

Jacob used an allegory given by the prophet Zenos to compare the house of Israel to "a tame olive tree" situated within a large vineyard of other olive trees (Jacob 5:3). In the allegory, God, the "tree surgeon," works painstakingly to help the tree bring forth its delicious natural fruit. Frustratingly, God's best efforts rarely result in His desired outcome. But God *never* gives up on the tree!

I love to read Zenos's allegory of the olive tree as a prophecy about the future destiny of The Church of Jesus Christ of Latter-day Saints. In the ongoing Restoration, God is devotedly trying to prune, graft, and develop His Church to bring forth the purest spiritual truths possible. There may be times when "wild fruit" (Jacob 5:25) manifests itself in the Church, but if we emulate the Master Arborist, we too will never give up on God's Church! Instead, we will "labor diligently with our might in the vineyard, that we may prepare the way, that [God] may bring forth again the natural fruit" (verse 61). When Jesus returns to earth, He will *fully* restore the beautiful natural fruits of God's Church. What a season that will be (see verses 71–76)!

TALKING POINT

In conjunction with your study of Jacob 5 this week, read and study Elder Jeffrey R. Holland's talk "The Grandeur of God." Consider what truths we learn about God's character and purposes from the allegory of the olive tree.

APR 15–21: "HE WORKETH IN ME TO DO ACCORDING TO HIS WILL"

ENOS–WORDS OF MORMON

Enos 1:10 (emphasis added)

> And while I was thus struggling in the spirit, behold, the voice of the Lord came into my mind again, saying: *I will visit thy brethren according to their diligence in keeping my commandments. I have given unto them this land, and it is a holy land; and I curse it not save it be for the cause of iniquity; wherefore, I will visit thy brethren according as I have said; and their transgressions will I bring down with sorrow upon their own heads.*

Promptings or my own thoughts? That seems to always be the question. Learning and discerning the voice of the Spirit is like learning a new language—difficult and often confusing. So how do we recognize promptings from the Holy Ghost?

Elder Quentin L. Cook describes the voice of the Spirit in this way: "Although its impact can be incredibly powerful, it most often comes quietly as a still, small voice. The scriptures include many examples of how the Spirit influences our minds, including speaking peace to our minds, occupying our minds, enlightening our minds, and even sending a voice to our minds" ("The Blessing of Continuing Revelation to Prophets and Personal Revelation to Guide Our Lives," *Ensign* or *Liahona*, May 2020).

Personal revelation is personal. How one person receives answers or direction can differ from another. I have friends who receive revelation in dreams. Others hear God's voice clearly as they read scriptures. No matter if it is through a still, small voice or feelings of peace, God wants to talk to His children. There may be moments when we receive direct and powerful messages, but there will also be times when heaven feels distant and closed off. But if we, like Enos, are diligent in keeping commandments and petitioning heaven, the voice of the Lord will *come again.*

TALKING POINT

Make a list of all the ways in which you hear God's voice. Consider past experiences, such as talking with other people, listening to music, feeling a sense of joy, receiving visions, or heeding whispers and promptings.

APR 22–28: "FILLED WITH LOVE TOWARDS GOD AND ALL MEN"

MOSIAH 1–3

Mosiah 3:19

> *For the natural man is an enemy to God, and has been from the fall of Adam, and will be, forever and ever, unless he yields to the enticings of the Holy Spirit, and putteth off the natural man and becometh a saint through the atonement of Christ the Lord, and becometh as a child, submissive, meek, humble, patient, full of love, willing to submit to all things which the Lord seeth fit to inflict upon him, even as a child doth submit to his father.*

There is a false sectarian notion referred to as "total depravity" that implies all people are naturally and inescapably predisposed to do evil. King Benjamin famously refers to "the natural man" as being an enemy to God (Mosiah 3:19). If we are not careful to understand the doctrine of this teaching, we might inadvertently begin to believe that God's children are innately evil instead of eternally and infinitely good.

Brigham Young tried to clarify what King Benjamin meant by "the natural man." President Young taught, "The natural man is of God. We are the natural sons and daughters of our natural parents, and spiritually we are the natural children of the Father of light and natural heirs to his kingdom; and when we do an evil, we do it in opposition to the promptings of the Spirit of Truth that is within us" (in *Journal of Discourses*, 9:305).

When viewed through the clarifying lens of Restoration theology, "the natural man" becomes a description of any one of us when we choose *not* to be true to who we *naturally* are—"sons and daughters of heavenly parents" (Russell M. Nelson, "'Thou Shalt Have No Other Gods,'" *Ensign*, May 1996). The more we "[yield] to the enticings of the Holy Spirit" (Mosiah 3:19), the more clearly we will see ourselves and others as innately good, naturally inclined to light, and "partakers of the divine nature" (2 Peter 1:4).

TALKING POINT

This week, see how many times you can look at someone and say in your mind, "That person is naturally good." Take note of how this affects your perception of humanity.

APR 29–MAY 5: "A MIGHTY CHANGE"

MOSIAH 4–6

Mosiah 4:27

And see that all these things are done in wisdom and order; for it is not requisite that a man should run faster than he has strength. And again, it is expedient that he should be diligent, that thereby he might win the prize; therefore, all things must be done in order.

When God commands us to do everything in "wisdom and order," what does that mean? Consider the rest of the verse. It includes the guideline to not "run faster than [we] have strength" for. But in our effort to do good, be Christlike, and "win the prize," we may find ourselves running too fast and losing strength doing it.

One way to stay "in wisdom" is to see our responsibilities not just as to-do lists but as stewardships. This particular mindset invites God to be a part of putting our daily doing in order so we walk more and run less.

In my book *The Stewardship Principle*, I explain what viewing our responsibilities as stewardships looks like. Here's an example: "Stewarding over your calendar means taking the opportunity to return and report every morning and night to a loving Father, in the name of His Beloved Son, with the aid of the Spirit. This pattern of accounting expands the possibilities that no day is wasted even if time was not fully maximized. Tomorrow, time will be afforded to you again. If this is your season of crying babies, blown tires, and missed appointments, remember that nothing is wasted in the economy of the Lord. The scriptures declare 'there is a season, and a time to every purpose under the heaven.' Do the best you can with the time you have been allotted" (American Fork: Covenant Communications, 2022, 15–16).

Wisdom is about trusting the order of not only our busy days but also the seasons of life. Letting go of what we thought needed doing and inviting God to be a part of both trimming the lawn and temple attendance. When we plan in this heavenly way, burnout will be lessened, and we will feel strengthened through Christ.

TALKING POINT

Saying no allows you to say yes to something else; it's okay to say no. In the spirit of being a wise steward and not running faster than you have strength, consider saying no to something this week so you can say yes to something else.

MAY 6–12: "IN THE STRENGTH OF THE LORD"

MOSIAH 7–10

Mosiah 8:16

> *And Ammon said that a seer is a revelator and a prophet also; and a gift which is greater can no man have, except he should possess the power of God, which no man can; yet a man may have great power given him from God.*

What would you say is the greatest blessing of being a member of The Church of Jesus Christ of Latter-day Saints? I'm sure you could come up with a long list. When Ammon discovered the people of King Limhi, he taught them specifically about the blessing of having access to a seer. Ammon explained that "a seer is a revelator and a prophet" and "can know of things which are past, and also of things which are to come, and . . . things which are not known shall be made known by them" (Mosiah 8:16–17).

Since the creation of the earth, God has mercifully used prophets, seers, and revelators to guide and direct His children. In the New Testament, the Apostle Paul taught Church members that one of the greatest blessings of belonging to the true Church of Jesus Christ was having access to what Paul referred to as "the oracles of God," referring to prophets and scriptures (Romans 3:1–2). Similarly, in the Book of Mormon, Ammon emphasized to King Limhi and his people that living prophets provide "a great benefit to [their] fellow beings" (Mosiah 8:18).

Through living prophets and apostles, God directs the Church. Conditions in the world will continue to change as we wait for the Second Coming of Jesus Christ. Thankfully,

TALKING POINT

Are you actively listening for the messages that God is trying to send to you *personally* through His living prophets and apostles? This week, study recent general conference addresses while actively asking God to speak to you. Be sure to record your impressions.

we can rest assured that God has always spoken, and will continue to speak, through designated seers to help us prepare for "things which are to come" (Mosiah 8:17).

MAY 13–19: "A LIGHT . . . THAT CAN NEVER BE DARKENED"

MOSIAH 11–17

Mosiah 15:7

Yea, even so he shall be led, crucified, and slain, the flesh becoming subject even unto death, the will of the Son being swallowed up in the will of the Father.

One of my favorite Christlike attributes is willingness. The Savior is eternally willing to have His will swallowed up in the Father's. He surrendered to pain and death so that we can overcome pain and death. Christ's Atonement is the ultimate example of letting God prevail.

President Russell M. Nelson recently taught about letting God prevail—being willing to submit to His will and see His power work in our lives. He asked many poignant questions that are worth pondering: "Are *you* willing to let God prevail in your life? Are *you* willing to let God be the most important influence in your life? Will you allow His words, His commandments, and His covenants to influence what you do each day? Will you allow His voice to take priority over any other? Are you *willing* to let whatever He needs you to do take precedence over every other ambition? Are you *willing* to have your will swallowed up in His?" ("Let God Prevail," *Ensign* or *Liahona*, November 2020).

When we surrender our will, we open ourselves up to let God prevail in our lives. We may not be asked, as the Savior was, to die for a cause, but as disciples of Christ, we have been asked to willingly give our lives to help build His kingdom. The amazing result is that whenever God asks for our sacrifice, He always gives back more in return. Thus the surrender of our will opens us up to more, not less.

God's prophet has invited us to recall and ponder on how God has previously prevailed in our lives and how He *will yet again* prevail in our lives. It is a promise from God. And when God says it, He keeps His promises. . . .

God is ready to facilitate mighty miracles in your behalf. (See Ganel-Lyn Condie, *When You Let God Prevail, His Promises Are Sure*, [American Fork: Covenant Communications, 2021], 2.)

TALKING POINT

How have you seen God prevail in your life this week? Where can you surrender your will and unlock heavenly power in your life?
Share your list with a loved one.

MAY 20–26: WE HAVE ENTERED INTO A COVENANT WITH HIM

MOSIAH 18–24

Mosiah 18:10

> *Now I say unto you, if this be the desire of your hearts, what have you against being baptized in the name of the Lord, as a witness before him that ye have entered into a covenant with him, that ye will serve him and keep his commandments, that he may pour out his Spirit more abundantly upon you?*

Do you remember when you were baptized? More importantly, do you remember the covenants you made when you were baptized? I can't think of anywhere in the scriptures where our baptismal covenants are explained as clearly as when Alma explained them in Mosiah 18.

Prior to the prophet Alma's conversion, he lived exclusively for his own comfort and welfare in the courts of King Noah (see Mosiah 23:9–11). But when Alma was baptized, all of that changed—he covenanted with God to live exclusively for the comfort and welfare of *others*. In short, he covenanted through baptism to be a true disciple of Jesus Christ.

So it is with us! Anyone who has been baptized has covenanted "to bear one another's burdens, . . . to mourn with those that mourn; yea, and comfort those that stand in need of comfort, and to stand as witnesses of God at all times and in all things" (Mosiah 18:8–9). True disciples of Jesus Christ live a life that is focused on *others*, not themselves. Elder Ronald A. Rasband said simply, "The scriptures describe that Jesus 'went about doing good.' So must we" ("To Heal the World," *Liahona*, May 2022).

TALKING POINT

The next time you partake of the sacrament, commit to God that you will try to not focus on yourself in the coming week. Then ask God to use you as an instrument in His hands to bless the lives of others in any way He sees fit. Be sure to journal about your experiences!

MAY 27–JUN 2: "THEY WERE CALLED THE PEOPLE OF GOD"

MOSIAH 25–28

Mosiah 27:31

> *Yea, every knee shall bow, and every tongue confess before him. Yea, even at the last day, when all men shall stand to be judged of him, then shall they confess that he is God; then shall they confess, who live without God in the world, that the judgment of an everlasting punishment is just upon them; and they shall quake, and tremble, and shrink beneath the glance of his all-searching eye.*

As a young child, I remember having a very childlike faith. I knew Jesus in a personal way and wanted everyone I loved to know Him that way too. Even as a child, I realized that not everyone believed as I did. I remember imagining all my elementary school teachers with me when Jesus comes again. I visualized all of us gathered together, waiting for and welcoming the Second Coming. In my innocence, I wholeheartedly anticipated the day, after Jesus's triumphant return, when my loved ones would all say, "Oh, you were right. He is real, He is here!"

Speaking of the glorious return of the Savior, Elder Neal A. Maxwell said, "Then the galleries and the mortal thrones will be empty. Even the great and spacious building will fall—and resoundingly! (see 1 Ne. 8:26–28). Then, too, those who have lived without God in the world will confess that God is God! (see Mosiah 27:31). Meanwhile, His character and attributes should evoke adoration and emulation from us" ("The Tugs and Pulls of the World," *Ensign*, November 2000).

TALKING POINT

Consider journaling or creating art about how you feel about the eventual Second Coming of the Savior. What might you feel or see on that wonderful day?

I can't wait for this wonderful day. My loved ones will be there—and so will yours! No matter where they are today, the promises are sure. As Mosiah says, all knees will bend before the Lord (see Mosiah 27:31). What a glorious reunion that will be!

JUN 3–9: "THEY WERE STEADFAST AND IMMOVABLE"

MOSIAH 29–ALMA 4

Alma 1:12

> *But Alma said unto him: Behold, this is the first time that priestcraft has been introduced among this people. And behold, thou art not only guilty of priestcraft, but hast endeavored to enforce it by the sword; and were priestcraft to be enforced among this people it would prove their entire destruction.*

Whenever someone teaches truth for the purpose of making *themselves* look and feel better, the scriptures refer to that as priestcraft. Nephi said that "priestcrafts are that men preach and set themselves up for a light unto the world, that they may get gain and praise of the world; but they seek not the welfare of Zion" (2 Nephi 26:29). Have you ever done or said the right things only so that you would look good?

Alma the Younger encountered a man named Nehor who proclaimed to be teaching the word of God, but his motives were all wrong. Nehor taught that people should "lift up their heads and rejoice; for the Lord had created all men, and had also redeemed all men" (Alma 1:4). That's certainly not satanic teaching! But Nehor's *motives* behind his teachings were all focused on self-aggrandizement and were not for the benefit of others and the building of God's kingdom (see Alma 1:3, 6).

We can all learn a valuable lesson from Nehor about the whys behind our righteous words and actions. Elder Gene R. Cook once gave an address in which he emphasized the importance of maintaining pure motives and staying focused on the welfare of others so that "it will be evident whom [the teacher] represents" ("Spiritual Guides for Teachers of Righteousness," *Ensign*, May 1982). In all we do, let us strive to be instruments in God's hands to accomplish His work, and give *Him* all the glory!

TALKING POINT

Take some time this week to sit and ponder the various whys behind your daily choices. Ask God to help you see how you can purify your motives so that your words and actions will more accurately reflect Jesus Christ and the beauties of His everlasting gospel.

Supplemental Study Help
Scan the QR code to access Gene R. Cook's talk "Spiritual Guides for Teachers of Righteousness."

JUN 10–16: "HAVE YE EXPERIENCED THIS MIGHTY CHANGE IN YOUR HEARTS?"

ALMA 5–7

Alma 5:14

> *And now behold, I ask of you, my brethren of the church, have ye spiritually been born of God? Have ye received his image in your countenances? Have ye experienced this mighty change in your hearts?*

I was diagnosed with a heart condition, which was caused by my lupus, over thirty-two years ago. There have been times when the physical pain in my chest was intense, and then there have been times when the scar tissue created a residual, consistent ache. Over the years, my chronic illness has taught me a lot about turning to God. I have tried to see Him in my life and receive more of His Spirit so I can bear the pain and the unknown—and be sanctified through Christ's grace. I have been changed by this challenging stewardship. My heart may not be as strong physically as it once was, but it is stronger spiritually.

As we invite God into the mundane and menacing aspects of our mortal journey, we will experience the "mighty change of heart" spoken of by Alma (Alma 5:14).

Elder Gerrit W. Gong taught about the blessings that come to us when we have a change of heart and draw nearer to the Savior. He said, "As our hearts change and we receive His image in our countenance, we see Him and ourselves in His Church. In Him, we find clarity, not dissonance. In Him, we find cause to do good, reason to be good, and increasing capacity to become better. In Him, we discover abiding faith, liberating selflessness, caring change, and trust in God" ("Room in the Inn," *Liahona*, May 2021).

The pain of life is a precious place to see God's image, because while we experience our own suffering, our capacity to empathize with others can increase. As we turn to the Savior for strength, we can receive His countenance and have our hearts changed. And as our hearts change, we will change our thoughts and actions toward those around us.

TALKING POINT

As we serve one another, we receive the image of God upon us and recognize it in others. Identify someone in your community, ward, or family who is navigating a chronic illness. Reach out and ask what support may look like for them.

JUN 17–23: JESUS CHRIST WILL COME TO REDEEM HIS PEOPLE

ALMA 8–12

Alma 9:28

Therefore, prepare ye the way of the Lord, for the time is at hand that all men shall reap a reward of their works, according to that which they have been—if they have been righteous they shall reap the salvation of their souls, according to the power and deliverance of Jesus Christ; and if they have been evil they shall reap the damnation of their souls, according to the power and captivation of the devil.

How far would you go to help a rebellious family member or friend avoid suffering? God never rests in His efforts to help His children enjoy His love and peace. While many people would give up on trying to help rebellious people avoid future suffering, God never does!

In the Book of Mormon, the people of Ammonihah vehemently rejected the prophet Alma's invitation to be baptized unto repentance (see Alma 8:9–13). Full of sorrow, Alma was simply going to move on. But God, knowing the calamities to come, directed him back to Ammonihah to preach a message of healing to His rebellious children. Alma declared upon his return, "The Son of God shall come . . . full of grace, equity, and truth, full of patience, mercy, and long-suffering, quick to hear the cries of his people and to answer their prayers" (Alma 9:26).

The people of Ammonihah again rejected Alma's loving warning, but in a way, that's beside the point. I see a lesson about how God will never give up on His children. As He said through Alma, "Whosoever repenteth, and hardeneth not his

TALKING POINT

Who in your life do you feel directed to love, guide, or warn? In your prayers this week, ask God to direct you to know how best to help a struggling family member or friend feel the reality of the Savior's love for them.

heart, he shall have claim on mercy through mine Only Begotten Son, unto a remission of his sins; and these shall enter into my rest" (Alma 12:34).

JUN 24–30: "ENTER INTO THE REST OF THE LORD"

ALMA 13–16

Alma 13:3

> *And this is the manner after which they were ordained— being called and prepared from the foundation of the world according to the foreknowledge of God, on account of their exceeding faith and good works; in the first place being left to choose good or evil; therefore they having chosen good, and exercising exceedingly great faith, are called with a holy calling, yea, with that holy calling which was prepared with, and according to, a preparatory redemption for such.*

I loved training to be an elementary school teacher and teaching kids at several grade levels. I did my student teaching in a first-grade class. Teaching first graders is amazing because first graders experience so much growth in just one school year. Many start the year as non-readers and then gain the skills and tools needed to put sounds, words, and sentences together, becoming master readers.

Often, parents are concerned when their child isn't progressing as fast as others. I would always encourage parents of my students to wait and see where their child was at by the end of first grade before doing any big interventions. Ninety percent of the time, we would see a non-reader catch up. So it is with our own eternal progression.

Alma 13:3 points to the "kindergarten" instruction we received before this earth life.

We learned the building blocks needed for "reading" before we got to earth. As we move through life, we continue learning—and becoming like our Heavenly Parents in the process. Some of us go forward through mortality with apparent ease and confidence, while some of us stumble and struggle.

Life can sometimes be plain hard. Simple as that. But something we can take comfort in is that we knew it would be hard and still chose to come. We were prepared with the knowledge and skills we needed to endure. Sister Elaine S. Dalton taught, "We knew that our earthly missions would be fraught with temptation, challenges, and hardship, but we also knew that we would be blessed by the fulness of the gospel, living prophets, and the guidance of the Holy Ghost" ("Look toward Eternity!," *Ensign* or *Liahona*, November 2006).

TALKING POINT

If you have received your patriarchal blessing, read it this week and highlight places where your spiritual gifts and promised blessings are mentioned. Make special note of any references to the premortal existence.

Some school years are harder than others, but with heavenly tutors and Christ as the merciful Teacher, we can stand confident in our eventual graduation.

JUL 1–7: "I WILL MAKE AN INSTRUMENT OF THEE"

ALMA 17–22

Alma 19:6

> *Now, this was what Ammon desired, for he knew that king Lamoni was under the power of God; he knew that the dark veil of unbelief was being cast away from his mind, and the light which did light up his mind, which was the light of the glory of God, which was a marvelous light of his goodness— yea, this light had infused such joy into his soul, the cloud of darkness having been dispelled, and that the light of everlasting life was lit up in his soul, yea, he knew that this had overcome his natural frame, and he was carried away in God.*

Imagine how inaccurately people would characterize you if they decided to judge you solely by your worst moments. In Alma 19, King Lamoni was in a spiritual coma for two days and nights. Some people declared that the king's body stunk and that he was dead and needed to be buried. But the king's wife said to Ammon, "As for myself, to me he doth not stink" (Alma 19:5). Where some people saw a decomposing dead body that needed to be buried, the faithful queen saw someone who simply needed God's touch to bring him back to life. Ammon assessed the king's condition and verified, "He is not dead, but he sleepeth in God, and on the morrow he shall rise again; therefore bury him not" (verse 8).

This world is full of people in spiritual comas. It's easy to look at those whose sins are more public than others and talk about how much they stink. It's easy to write them off and not try to spiritually revive them. But if we follow the example of this faithful queen, then we will never lose hope for any soul to awaken unto God.

Consider what the queen did and think about how you can minister to those who are spiritually sleeping or lost: "And it came to pass that she watched over the bed of her husband, from that time even until that time on the morrow which Ammon had appointed that he should rise" (Alma 19:11). The next day, the king arose as an unflinching disciple of Jesus Christ. President Dallin H. Oaks taught, "The power of the Atonement and the principle of repentance show that we should never give up on loved ones who now seem to be making many wrong choices" ("The Challenge to Become," *Ensign*, November 2000).

TALKING POINT

Is there anyone in your life who you have given up on prematurely? Besides the queen in Alma 19, what scripture characters and teachings in this week's reading give you hope for those who are spiritually asleep?

JUL 8–14: THEY "NEVER DID FALL AWAY"

ALMA 23–29

Alma 29:1

O that I were an angel, and could have the wish of mine heart, that I might go forth and speak with the trump of God, with a voice to shake the earth, and cry repentance unto every people!

In a world saturated with social media, there are a lot of voices sharing advice: what to wear, what to buy, how to find happiness, and so much more. Everyone seems to have their own trumpet to shout their messages and opinions to the world.

What would the Book of Mormon prophets have done with social media? I think Alma would have done his best to use it for good and to share the gospel. He wished that he could "speak with the trump of God, with a voice to shake the earth" (Alma 29:2).

Elder Neal A. Maxwell said,

> Alma urgently desired to be the "trump of God" so that he might "shake the earth" (Alma 29:1). But *not because of ego*; in fact, Alma wanted to declare repentance and the plan of redemption to all mankind so that there might be no more human sorrow (see Alma 29:2). . . .
>
> Thus becoming content with his calling, Alma then meekly hoped to be an instrument to help save some soul (see Alma 29:9). ("Content with the Things Allotted unto Us," *Ensign*, May 2000; emphasis added)

No matter what people are promoting on social media, the thing that will make us the most happy is the gospel of Jesus Christ. How can you use your voice to spread positivity and touch the lives of others with your testimony of the Savior?

TALKING POINT

How are we using our "trumpets"? What messages are you sharing with the world? Consider posting a faith-focused message on social media this week.

JUL 15–21: "THE VIRTUE OF THE WORD OF GOD"

ALMA 30–31

Alma 31:32–33

O Lord, wilt thou comfort my soul, and give unto me success, and also my fellow laborers who are with me. . . . Yea, wilt thou comfort their souls in Christ.

Wilt thou grant unto them that they may have strength, that they may bear their afflictions which shall come upon them because of the iniquities of this people.

I honestly have no idea *how* prayer actually works, but I know from experience that it does! When Alma and his companions went on a mission to the apostate Zoramites, Alma was overwhelmed with what he saw. He knew that if he and his friends were going to be successful in their missionary efforts, they would need God's help. So Alma turned to prayer.

TALKING POINT

While reading Alma 31, look for examples of effective and ineffective prayers. Then study President Nelson's talk "Sweet Power of Prayer" and consider how you can increase the power of your own prayers.
Scan the QR code to access President Nelson's talk.

Among other things, Alma prayed for strength to bear his infirmities and for God to comfort his soul in Christ (see Alma 31:30–31). He also prayed that his mission companions would receive the same blessings (see Alma 31:32–33). Alma 31:38 describes the result of Alma's faithful prayer: "And the Lord provided for them that they should hunger not, neither should they thirst; yea, and he also gave them strength, that they should suffer no manner of afflictions, save it were swallowed up in the joy of Christ. *Now this was according to the prayer of Alma; and this because he prayed in faith*" (emphasis added).

Like Alma, we can also access what President Russell M. Nelson once referred to as "the sweet power of prayer" (see "Sweet Power of Prayer," *Ensign* or *Liahona*, May 2003). Alma's prayer of faith brought blessings into his life and the lives of those he loved. Our prayers of faith will result in the same blessings!

JUL 22–28: "PLANT THIS WORD IN YOUR HEARTS"

ALMA 32–35

Alma 32:28

> *Now, we will compare the word unto a seed. Now, if ye give place, that a seed may be planted in your heart, behold, if it be a true seed, or a good seed, if ye do not cast it out by your unbelief, that ye will resist the Spirit of the Lord, behold, it will begin to swell within your breasts; and when you feel these swelling motions, ye will begin to say within yourselves—It must needs be that this is a good seed, or that the word is good, for it beginneth to enlarge my soul; yea, it beginneth to enlighten my understanding, yea, it beginneth to be delicious to me.*

I am not a scientist by nature, but I am grateful God has given His children the opportunity to experiment upon His word—to evaluate and analyze it. As a wise and loving Father, He wants us to learn for ourselves.

As we study the gospel, we can progress along the path of conversion. Alma 32:28 gives us the formula for the experiment. Step one is to have a desire and then plant our seed of faith. We can't stop there, hoping that watering our seed with the occasional prayer or study session will keep it alive. The next steps are to consistently nourish and protect our belief with patience and care. The inevitable heat of the day will come—maybe in the form of doubt, ridicule, or the occasional anti-faith social media post. When this happens, don't dig up your seed or leave your growing plant to wither away. Then comes the important step of continuing to experiment upon God's word and seek support from faithful friends.

What will the final result of this experiment be? A beautiful tree and an equally beautiful testimony, confirmed by the power of the Holy Ghost, which will "begin to swell within your breasts" and help you conclude that "the word is good" (Alma 32:28). That's the power of experimenting on the word. As Sister Barbara Thompson said, "As we seek answers to our questions, [God] will bless us with His Spirit" ("Personal Revelation and Testimony," *Ensign* or *Liahona*, November 2011).

TALKING POINT

Identify one gospel principle you are struggling with. Consider planting a seed of faith and find ways to consistently nourish it for the next thirty days. Knowing that the heat of the day will come, find ways to cast out unbelief and protect the small sprout of faith you see growing. After thirty days, evaluate how you have changed and how you feel. What witnesses from the Spirit have you experienced?

65

JUL 29–AUG 4: "LOOK TO GOD AND LIVE"

ALMA 36–38

Alma 36:24

Yea, and from that time even until now, I have labored without ceasing, that I might bring souls unto repentance; that I might bring them to taste of the exceeding joy of which I did taste; that they might also be born of God, and be filled with the Holy Ghost.

Shame and guilt are not synonymous. Shame is a tool of the adversary, a lie that tells us we are worthless because of our sins. Guilt, on the other hand, "is to our spirit what pain is to our body—a warning of danger and a protection from additional damage" (David A. Bednar, "We Believe in Being Chaste," *Ensign* or *Liahona*, May 2013). Shame is destructive and keeps us in spiritual bondage; guilt helps us recognize sin and avoid it.

> ## TALKING POINT
> Journal this week about the differences between shame and guilt, and consider the role that each has played and continues to play in your life. Pray each day for the ability to recognize and overcome moments when you are held captive by shame.

Alma seemed to think that God would never forgive him or want to have a meaningful relationship with him because of his sins (see Alma 36:14–15). That false and shame-ridden belief sent Alma into a dark spiritual coma for three days and nights. Those three days were not punishment for Alma; that's how long it took him to finally experience Jesus Christ's atoning grace and escape Satan's shackles of shame.

After his three days of suffocating shame, Alma said, "I remembered . . . Jesus Christ" and "I cried within my heart: O Jesus, thou Son of God, have mercy on me" (Alma 36:17–18). Immediately, Alma "could remember [his] pains no more," and "[his] soul was filled with joy as exceeding as was [his] pain!" (Alma 36:19–20). The Savior freed Alma from shame.

Alma's experience helps us see that God never uses shame to motivate His children—He takes shame away! God does, however, allow the natural consequences of our sins (guilt) to teach us the valuable lessons of mortality.

AUG 5–11: "THE GREAT PLAN OF HAPPINESS"

ALMA 39–42

Alma 41:10

> *Do not suppose, because it has been spoken concerning restoration, that ye shall be restored from sin to happiness. Behold, I say unto you, wickedness never was happiness.*

Have you or another parent you know ever struggled to watch a child continuously choose things that don't make them happy? They eat too much candy and get sick. Or they take a friend's toy and it causes a fight. Basically anything where they choose the opposite of what they are guided to choose. And even after comfort and counsel, when the opportunity presents itself again, the child once again devours more sweets or fights with a sibling over a toy. Did they learn anything the first time?

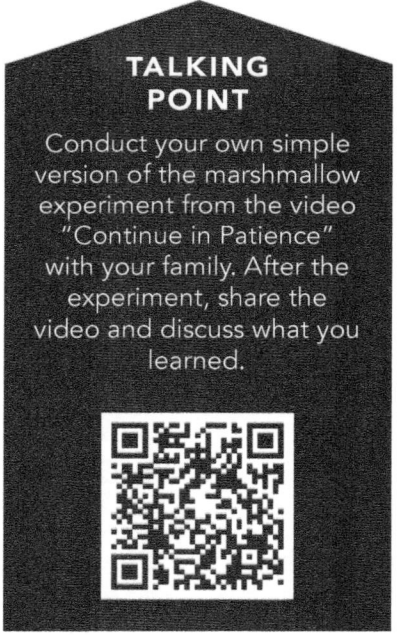

TALKING POINT

Conduct your own simple version of the marshmallow experiment from the video "Continue in Patience" with your family. After the experiment, share the video and discuss what you learned.

Even when we know what will truly make us happy, it's hard to make the right choice in the moment. The adversary is always tempting us to choose things that will bring us initial pleasure but then only lead to eternal misery. Juxtapose that with what our Heavenly Parents counsel us to do: obey commandments that call for delayed gratification but lead to forever happiness.

Even when we feel overwhelmed at the wrong choices we have made, we can remember that we are learning and growing. As Elder Dieter F. Uchtdorf taught, "We learn the important lessons of life through experience. Through learning from our mistakes. Through repenting

and realizing for ourselves that 'wickedness never was happiness'"
("Come and Belong," *Ensign* or *Liahona*, May 2020).

AUG 12–18: "STAND FAST IN THE FAITH OF CHRIST"

ALMA 43–52

Alma 48:17

> *Yea, verily, verily I say unto you, if all men had been, and were, and ever would be, like unto Moroni, behold, the very powers of hell would have been shaken forever; yea, the devil would never have power over the hearts of the children of men.*

A "pied piper" is someone who offers seductive and destructive enticements to others. Satan is a pied piper. He first binds his victims with soft, silky cords, filling them with a false sense of safety, and ensuring them that they are still in control. But soon those unthreatening silky cords become "strong cords" that bring about spiritual captivity (see 2 Nephi 26:22).

In Alma 47, we read about how the treacherous Amalickiah convinced the unwitting Lehonti to give up his high ground. Once vulnerable, Lehonti was secretly "[administered] poison by degrees" until he died, thus giving Amalickiah full control of the Lamanite armies.

In contrast to Lehonti stands Captain Moroni, "a strong and a mighty man; . . . a man who was firm in the faith of Christ" (Alma 48:11, 13). When pressured to give up his spiritual high ground and come down to the lowlands of corruption and evil, Captain Moroni fortified his spiritual location and actively encouraged others to do the same.

The scriptures tell us what the world would be like if we were all more like Captain Moroni and refused to give heed to the many pied pipers who strive daily to distract us: "The very powers of hell would [be] shaken forever; yea, the devil would never have power over the hearts of the children of men" (Alma 48:17).

TALKING POINT

Look for examples in this week's reading of individuals who stayed true to the standards of truth in the face of worldly opposition. In addition, read Elder Dieter F. Uchtdorf's talk "We Are Doing a Great Work and Cannot Come Down" to help you assess your own spiritual focus and commitment. Be sure to record your impressions. Scan the QR code to access Elder Uchtdorf's talk.

AUG 19–25: "PRESERVED BY HIS MARVELOUS POWER"

ALMA 53–63

Alma 56:47–48

Now they never had fought, yet they did not fear death; and they did think more upon the liberty of their fathers than they did upon their lives; yea, they had been taught by their mothers, that if they did not doubt, God would deliver them.

And they rehearsed unto me the words of their mothers, saying: We do not doubt our mothers knew it.

The story of the stripling warriors and their mothers has been used a lot as an example of good parenting. We may mistakenly believe that these mothers planned the best gospel discussions and home evening activities in order to raise such steadfast and unwavering sons. But if we look closer, we can see that faithful children don't come from perfect parents.

The backstory of the Anti-Nephi-Lehies shows that the mothers and fathers of the stripling warriors were recovering addicts. And yet, they raised their children with vulnerability and faith. They taught, preached, and spoke of Christ so their children would know what source to turn to when things were hard, scary, and uncertain (see 2 Nephi 25:26). Imperfect parents who have overcome hardship and sin know the joy of repentance and the redemptive power of God.

"Parents don't have to be perfect to raise great kids. This army of Helaman did not have perfect parents. They had parents who had repented, who had once been the enemy and then changed. The stripling warriors might have remembered their parents' past. When looking into the eyes of their mothers, they might have recalled the times their moms had taken care of the family because their dads were off fighting . . . again. These boys knew opposition and understood redemption because they had witnessed their parents' mighty change of heart. Goodly parents aren't perfect parents. They are just parents striving, trying, repenting, and trying some more" (Ganel-Lyn Condie, *Mother to Mother*, [American Fork: Covenant Communications, 2017], 9).

TALKING POINT

Children often believe their parents were never young and never made mistakes. What would happen if our kids heard about our own repentance process and could be strengthened in their trust that God will deliver them too? Consider opening up to a child or a loved one about a time you experienced Christ's redemption through repentance.

AUG 26–SEP 1: "THE ROCK OF OUR REDEEMER"

HELAMAN 1–6

Helaman 5:9

O remember, remember, my sons, . . . yea, remember that there is no other way nor means whereby man can be saved, only through the atoning blood of Jesus Christ, who shall come; yea, remember that he cometh to redeem the world.

The Leaning Tower of Pisa is famous for all the wrong reasons. The tower started to noticeably lean in 1178, five years into its construction. The unstable foundation of clay, sand, and shells unexpectedly settled, which created the lean that has only worsened over time. While it is a small miracle that the Tower of Pisa still stands, the regrettable destiny of this structure was set centuries ago when the first stone was laid on an unstable foundation.

Everyone needs a *spiritual* foundation checkup from time to time. President Russell M. Nelson said to members of the Church, "I ask each of you, how firm is *your* foundation? And what reinforcements to your testimony and understanding of the gospel are needed?" ("The Temple and Your Spiritual Foundation," *Liahona*, November 2021).

Helaman reminded his sons what is required for our spiritual foundations to remain firm in the midst of life's storms: "Remember, remember that it is upon the rock of our Redeemer, who is Christ, the Son of God, that ye must build your foundation; that when the devil shall send forth his mighty winds, yea, his shafts in the whirlwind, yea, when all his hail and his mighty storm shall beat upon you, it shall have no power over you to drag you down to the gulf of misery and

> **TALKING POINT**
>
> This week, perform a spiritual foundation checkup on yourself. What "stones" comprise your life's spiritual foundation, and what steps can you take to make Jesus Christ your foundation's "chief corner stone" (Ephesians 2:20)?

endless wo, because of the rock upon which ye are built, which is a sure foundation, a foundation whereon if men build they cannot fall" (Helaman 5:12).

SEP 2–8: "REMEMBER THE LORD"

HELAMAN 7–12

Helaman 12:2–3

Yea, and we may see at the very time when he doth prosper his people, . . . doing all things for the welfare and happiness of his people; yea, then is the time that they do harden their hearts, and do forget the Lord their God, and do trample under their feet the Holy One—yea, and this because of their ease, and their exceedingly great prosperity.

And thus we see that except the Lord doth chasten his people with many afflictions, yea, except he doth visit them with death and with terror, and with famine and with all manner of pestilence, they will not remember him.

Everyone carries some kind of burden in this life, such as the heavy loads of loss, longing, and limitations. Despite the pain of our challenges, we can take comfort in the fact that "God is love" (1 John 4:8) and that He wants us to be happy.

Looking at difficult stewardships as gifts instead of punishments can help us navigate life's ups and downs. It may be hard to view our burdens this way, but if we pay attention, we will see the blessings that come from them. Elder David A. Bednar taught, "Sometimes we mistakenly may believe that happiness is the absence of a load. But bearing a load is a necessary and essential part of the plan of happiness" ("Bear Up Their Burdens with Ease," *Ensign* or *Liahona*, May 2014).

It is natural to want peace and prosperity and to believe that is where happiness is found. But in reality, we often prosper while we are afflicted by various challenges. Muscles are built with weight. Trucks gain traction with heavier loads (see David A. Bednar, "Bear Up Their Burdens"). And sanctification comes in the season following serious struggles with our stewardships. This is a pattern for our growth, overseen by our loving and merciful Father. As we remember Him, He will continue to help us overcome and be strengthened by our trials.

TALKING POINT

This week, offer a prayer of gratitude for something difficult you have gone through. As you talk with God, consider how this burden helped you learn and grow.

SEP 9–15: "GLAD TIDINGS OF GREAT JOY"

HELAMAN 13–16

Helaman 16:13–14

But it came to pass . . . , there were great signs given unto the people, and wonders; and the words of the prophets began to be fulfilled.

And angels did appear unto men, wise men, and did declare unto them glad tidings of great joy; thus in this year the scriptures began to be fulfilled.

Have you ever wondered what the world will be like in the years leading up to Jesus's Second Coming? President Ezra Taft Benson said, "The record of the Nephite history just prior to the Savior's visit reveals many parallels to our own day as we anticipate the Savior's second coming" ("The Savior's Visit to America," *Ensign*, May 1987). Those Second Coming parallels can be found in the books of Helaman and 3 Nephi.

In the latter chapters of Helaman, we read of a world spiritually spiraling downward, but we also read about miraculous signs and wonders that preceded Christ's coming. So it is today! Many people seek for that which they cannot obtain—"[they] have sought for happiness in doing iniquity, which thing is contrary to the nature of that righteousness which is in our great and Eternal Head" (Helaman 13:38). But between now and the time Jesus returns, "we will see the *greatest* manifestations of the Savior's power that the world has *ever* seen" (Russell M. Nelson, "Overcome the World and Find Rest," *Liahona*, November 2022).

Fortunately, our level of spiritual preparedness for the Second Coming is up to us. As Samuel the Lamanite put it, "Ye can do good and be restored unto that which is good, . . . or ye can do evil, and have that which is evil restored unto you" (Helaman 14:31). Every time we consciously choose light over dark, we ready ourselves for the return of Jesus Christ.

TALKING POINT

Take on a Second Coming prayer challenge this week. At least once a day, pray and ask Heavenly Father to hasten the day of His Son's return. Then ask God what you can do to assist in ushering in the Second Coming of Jesus Christ. Record your impressions.

SEP 16–22: "LIFT UP YOUR HEAD AND BE OF GOOD CHEER"

3 NEPHI 1–7

3 Nephi 1:13

Lift up your head and be of good cheer; for behold, the time is at hand, and on this night shall the sign be given, and on the morrow come I into the world, to show unto the world that I will fulfil all that which I have caused to be spoken by the mouth of my holy prophets.

Whether we are naturally optimistic or pessimistic, the Lord wants us to experience joy and hope. Daily life can sometimes feel overwhelming and discouraging, but no matter what we are facing, the Savior invites us to "lift up [our] head and be of good cheer" (3 Nephi 1:13).

This is exactly what He told Nephi to do when his people were about to be murdered by nonbelievers for waiting for the promised sign

TALKING POINT

Make a list of moments in your life when you have experienced real joy despite struggles you were going through during those times. Share one of these experiences with a loved one or on social media and testify of how Christ made it possible.

of Jesus's birth. The natural thing for Nephi to do would have been to despair, but Jesus still invited him to trust just a little longer, to still anticipate "that day and that night and that day which should be as one day as if there were no night" (3 Nephi 1:8). So much in our daily life can feel overwhelming and discouraging, but in Christ, we can find help through our trials and a joy that passes understanding.

Elder Jonathan S. Schmitt said, "Today, as our world is frequently polarized and divided, there is a great need for us to preach and practice positivity, optimism, and hope. Despite any challenges in our past, faith always points toward the future, filled with hope, allowing us to fulfill Jesus's invitation to be of good cheer. Joyfully living the gospel helps us to become *disciples of good things to come*" ("That They Might Know Thee," *Liahona*, November 2022).

If you find yourself currently trapped in a trying time, keep your eyes on Jesus and choose to be of good cheer. Jesus has overcome all and is the ultimate source of joy when it seems like a scarce natural resource. He will help you through anything.

SEP 23–29: "ARISE AND COME FORTH UNTO ME"

3 NEPHI 8–11

3 Nephi 11:15

And it came to pass that the multitude went forth, and thrust their hands into his side, and did feel the prints of the nails in his hands and in his feet; and this they did do, going forth one by one until they had all gone forth, and did see with their eyes and did feel with their hands, and did know of a surety and did bear record, that it was he, of whom it was written by the prophets, that should come.

Jesus Christ will come again! Let that reality sink deep into your heart. There are many beliefs about what that day will be like, but I believe the Savior's Second Coming will *primarily* be characterized by a profound and absolute knowledge that God knows us individually.

When Jesus appeared to roughly 2,500 people in the Book of Mormon following His Resurrection, His first item of business was to have a one-on-one moment with every individual. That would have taken a long time. But Jesus seems to have wanted each of these people to know Him, and, perhaps more importantly, for them to know that *He* knew *them*.

Elder Dieter F. Uchtdorf said,

> God knows you. . . . This very day—every day—He reaches out to you, desiring to heal you, to lift you up, and to replace the emptiness in your heart with an abiding joy. He desires to sweep away any darkness that clouds your life and fill it with the sacred and brilliant light of His unending glory. ("Believe, Love, Do," *Ensign* or *Liahona*, November 2018)

When Jesus Christ returns, we will each come to know how perfectly He knows and loves us. That experience will cause us all to cry out like the Nephites, "Hosanna! Blessed be the name of the Most High God!" (3 Nephi 11:17). Then we will fall at Jesus's feet, worship Him, and bask in His love and healing. What a wonderful day that will be!

TALKING POINT

What evidence can you point to in your life that shows God knows you personally? Make a list of both general and specific things that prove you are perfectly known by God, then record how this makes you feel.

Supplemental Study Help
Scan the QR code to access Elder C. Scott Grow's talk "And This Is Life Eternal."

SEP 30–OCT 6: "I AM THE LAW, AND THE LIGHT"

3 NEPHI 12–16

3 Nephi 12:48

Therefore I would that ye should be perfect even as I, or your Father who is in heaven is perfect.

The scriptures command us to be perfect like our Father in heaven is, but how is that possible?

The Savior's invitation to be perfect, if not understood correctly, can make us feel like we will never measure up, or like we'll have to do more than we can reasonably manage to ever make it. But maybe thinking about this in terms of what we can do isn't the point—what if, instead, we thought about what Christ can do to help us? "True followers of Christ may become perfect through His grace and Atonement" (Guide to the Scriptures, "Perfect," scriptures. ChurchofJesusChrist.org). Understanding that Jesus is the way, the only way, to become perfected can help us reduce feelings of being overwhelmed, discouragement, and comparisons.

Elder Paul V. Johnson taught, "We may have a tendency to think we have to perfect ourselves, but that is not possible. Following every suggestion in every self-help book in the world will not bring it about. There is only one way and one name whereby perfection comes. We are 'made perfect through Jesus the mediator of the new covenant, who wrought out this perfect atonement through the shedding of his own blood.' Our perfection is only possible through God's grace" ("Be Perfected in Him," *Liahona*, November 2022).

This life is a time of becoming, but we will never be whole or complete until Jesus comes again. So until that glorious day, let us press forward, relying on Christ to give us the power to reach our eventual perfection.

TALKING POINT

President Lorenzo Snow taught the importance of striving for perfection in a reasonable way. He said, "Do not expect to become perfect at once. If you do, you will be disappointed. Be better today than you were yesterday, and be better tomorrow than you are today. . . . Thus continue to be a little better day by day" (*Teachings of Presidents of the Church: Lorenzo Snow* [2012], 103). What is one area of life where you can be just a little better today than you were yesterday? Actively seek to improve in this area each day this week.

85

OCT 7–13: "BEHOLD, MY JOY IS FULL"

3 NEPHI 17–19

3 Nephi 17:9

And it came to pass that when he had thus spoken, all the multitude, with one accord, did go forth with their sick and their afflicted, and their lame, and with their blind, and with their dumb, and with all them that were afflicted in any manner; and he did heal them every one as they were brought forth unto him.

Jesus is sometimes referred to as the Great Physician. Wherever He goes, healing goes with Him. If you or someone you love could be healed of anything right now, what would it be? When Jesus visited the Nephites, He said, "Have ye any that are sick among you? Bring them hither. Have ye any that are . . . afflicted in any manner? Bring them hither and I will heal them" (3 Nephi 17:7). As people came unto the Savior, "he did heal them every one" (verse 9).

My daughter is intellectually disabled and nonverbal. She can communicate with sounds and gestures, but she can't talk. When Jesus Christ comes again, He will heal my daughter and make her whole. I can't wait until the first time she looks at me and says in perfect clarity, "Daddy!" When that happens, I will bow down in joy before Jesus and "bathe his feet with [my] tears" (3 Nephi 17:9–10).

TALKING POINT

Consider the personal ailments (physical *and* spiritual) for which *you* need the Savior's healing. Next, consider all of the healing you long to see in the lives of those you love. This week, try to picture the *reality* of what that healing will look like when Jesus comes again. Record your feelings and impressions.

Yes, Jesus can and will heal all physical ailments. But as incredible as that is, His physical miracles point to an even greater power—His ability to heal all *spiritual* ills. The *spiritually* blind and deaf and lame will also be healed and freed from Satan's grasp. I am sure that "eye hath never seen, neither hath the ear heard, before, so great and marvelous things" as we shall experience when Jesus comes again (3 Nephi 17:16).

OCT 14–20: "YE ARE THE CHILDREN OF THE COVENANT"

3 NEPHI 20–26

3 Nephi 20:26

The Father having raised me up unto you first, and sent me to bless you in turning away every one of you from his iniquities; and this because ye are the children of the covenant.

I am so grateful for covenants. When we keep covenants, they keep us. In today's world of "you do you," it is not always popular to be a covenant maker or keeper. So many of Satan's distractions discourage us from our discipleship. My son once counseled his soon-to-be-endowed sister, "When you make temple covenants, it may seem easy. But it is later, in keeping those same covenants, that you see the importance and the intensity required in maintaining them." Covenants and commandments are about our relationship with our Father in Heaven—a binding between God and His child. This verse of scripture testifies of the power to bless that comes only through becoming a covenant child of God.

Elder Bednar taught it so powerfully when he said,

> The Savior also taught the people to come unto Him through sacred covenants, and He reminded them that they were 'the children of the covenant' (3 Nephi 20:26). He emphasized the eternal importance of the ordinances of baptism (see 3 Nephi 11:19–39) and of receiving the Holy Ghost (see 3 Nephi 11:35–36; 12:6; 18:36–38). In a similar manner, you and I are admonished to turn toward and learn from Christ and to come unto Him through the covenants and ordinances of His restored gospel. As we do so, we will eventually and ultimately come to know Him (see John 17:3), 'in his own time, and in his own way, and according to his own will' (Doctrine and Covenants 88:68), as did the people in the land of Bountiful." ("Clean Hands and a Pure Heart," *Ensign* or *Liahona*, November 2007).

What beautiful promises. Ultimately, we can come to know God in intimate and personal ways through our covenants. Whether it is participating in temple ordinances or partaking of the sacrament, access to heavenly power is available on Earth today for all the Father's children. What a wonderful time to be alive. God has not sent us to Earth to struggle and stress on our own. He wants to be connected with us as we work out our mortality. And we make it eternally easier when we lean on and learn from Him through covenant making and keeping.

TALKING POINT

What is the next covenant on the path for you? How can you share the power and peace you have received from making covenants with someone who is also walking the covenant path? Consider visiting a temple and participating in ordinances. If needed, schedule an appointment with your bishop to make the necessary adjustments to move toward a temple recommend and attendance.

OCT 21–27: "THERE COULD NOT BE A HAPPIER PEOPLE"

3 NEPHI 27–4 NEPHI

4 Nephi 1:2

And it came to pass in the thirty and sixth year, the people were all converted unto the Lord, upon all the face of the land, both Nephites and Lamanites, and there were no contentions and disputations among them, and every man did deal justly one with another.

After Jesus Christ visited the Nephites, they enjoyed nearly 200 years of communal joy and peace. What was the key to their extended happiness and tranquility as a society? 4 Nephi gives us some specifics: "the people were all converted" (verse 2), "they had all things common among them" (verse 3), "the love of God . . . did dwell in [their] hearts" (verse 15), and "they were in one, the children of Christ" (verse 17). Any collective progress we want to see in society has to start with each of us.

The famous Three Nephites were among Jesus's disciples in the western hemisphere. Jesus asked the Three Nephites, "What is it that ye desire of me, after that I am gone to the Father?" (3 Nephi 28:1). Of all the *good* things they could have requested, they "desired that [they] might bring the souls of men unto [Christ], while the world shall stand" (verse 9). Because of their Christlike altruism, Jesus said, "Ye shall sit down in the kingdom of my Father; yea, your joy shall be full" (verse 10).

The key to living "after the manner of happiness" (2 Nephi 5:27) is living for others, putting others' comforts before our own. That's the way Jesus lived His life, that's the way the Three Nephites are *still* living their lives, and that's the way we each must learn to live if we hope to be a part of God's future millennial kingdom.

TALKING POINT

Begin creating a Zion-like society this week by looking for opportunities to anonymously put others' comforts before your own. Each time you consciously serve someone, take note of the peace and joy you feel. With each act of service, you are becoming more like the Savior and preparing the world for His return!

OCT 28–NOV 3: "I WOULD THAT I COULD PERSUADE ALL . . . TO REPENT"

MORMON 1–6

Mormon 5:11 (emphasis added)

For I know that such will sorrow for the calamity of the house of Israel; yea, they will sorrow for the destruction of this people; they will sorrow that this people had not repented that they might have been clasped in the arms of Jesus.

Repentance is about turning back to God and continuing to live righteously. It isn't about punishing ourselves. When we joyfully repent every day, we will not sorrow.

Sinning can be broadly defined as anything that separates us from God. When we sin, consequences may play out longer and be more uncomfortable than we want, but that doesn't change the power that repentance can have to make your life better. Don't add to your suffering by delaying your repentance.

"In the anguishing process of repentance, we may sometimes feel God has deserted us. The reality is that our behavior has isolated us from Him. Thus, while we are turning away from evil but have not yet turned fully to God, we are especially vulnerable. Yet we must not give up, but, instead, reach out to God's awaiting arm of mercy, which is outstretched 'all the day long.' (Jacob 5:47; Jacob 6:4; 2 Ne. 28:32; Morm. 5:11.) Unlike us, God has no restrictive office hours" (Neal A. Maxwell, "Repentance," *Ensign*, November 1991).

Ancient prophets like Mormon sorrowed because people chose

> **TALKING POINT**
>
> Daily, joyful repentance is a beautiful way to end every day. Tonight as you kneel in prayer, give an account to God for what you have done. Visualize a loving Father with outstretched arms. Don't be afraid to share your mistakes and regrets with Him.

not to repent. How often do we make repentance too complicated instead of reframing it and seeing it for what it really is? I love the idea that God is always there, reaching out an arm of mercy, hoping that we will fall into His ever-open embrace.

NOV 4–10: "I SPEAK UNTO YOU AS IF YE WERE PRESENT"

MORMON 7–9

Mormon 9:14

> **And then cometh the judgment of the Holy One upon them; and then cometh the time that he that is filthy shall be filthy still; and he that is righteous shall be righteous still; he that is happy shall be happy still; and he that is unhappy shall be unhappy still.**

We sometimes overanalogize earthly realities with heavenly truths. For example, when people try to understand the Final Judgment, they usually think of being the defendant in an earthly courtroom with an unbending judge. But a close reading of the scriptures and latter-day prophets challenges that analogy.

The prophet Mormon referenced "the day of judgment" (Mormon 7:10). He also emphasized that for anyone who chooses to come unto Jesus, judgment will be followed by "a state of happiness which hath no end" (verse 7). That makes me excited for the Final Judgment!

Moroni additionally encouraged us to "be wise in the days of [our] probation" (Mormon 9:28) because every one of our choices *immediately* makes us either *more* or *less* like God. In this way, "judgment" is an organic process happening to us every day with every choice we make. The Final Judgment is simply a checkpoint in our eternal journey where we observe how "the *condition* we have achieved" compares to the condition of the Savior. The Final Judgment is an opportunity to assess up to that point in our existence the "effect of our acts and thoughts—what we have *become*" (Dallin H. Oaks, "The Challenge to Become," *Ensign*, November 2000).

Our *eternal* lives obviously continue after the Final Judgment, and so will our agency. Thus, the sobering truth is that the *only* thing that will ever prevent me from becoming like God is *me* and the choices *I* choose to make, now and forever!

TALKING POINT

Remember that judgment is happening now. Each of our choices makes us more like God or less like God. Every night this week, sit down and review the choices you made that day. For each choice that you identify, ask yourself, "Did that choice increase or decrease the amount of light in my life?" Strive each day to choose light.

NOV 11–17: "REND THAT VEIL OF UNBELIEF"

ETHER 1–5

Ether 4:12 (emphasis added)

And whatsoever thing persuadeth men to do good is of me; for good cometh of none save it be of me. I am the same that leadeth men to all good; he that will not believe my words will not believe me—that I am; and he that will not believe me will not believe the Father who sent me. For behold, I am the Father, I am the light, and the life, and the truth of the world.

Have you ever been at a concert when all of a sudden someone in the audience turns on their cell phone flashlight and waves it in the air? Even though it's just one small light, it never goes unnoticed. And it usually starts a chain reaction—many others in the audience will join in with their phones as well. The end result is a beautiful sea of glittering light. Even though those individual lights are small, each one makes an incredible impact and clears away darkness.

Jesus is "the light, and the life, and the truth of the world" (Ether 4:12). Like a cell phone flashlight (but way more powerful), He helps us discern what is good and true through the power of the Holy Ghost. He can answer our questions.

Sister Sharon Eubank taught, "For those seeking truth, it may seem at first to be the foolish claustrophobia of windows made of stone. But with patience and faithful questions, Jesus can transform our windows of stone to glass and light. Christ is light to see" ("Christ: The Light That Shines in Darkness," *Ensign* or *Liahona*, May 2019).

TALKING POINT

One night this week, gather your family or some friends and turn off all the lights in your house, then light just one candle. Sit by the candle and listen to sacred music that connects you with the Savior. Share how focusing on Christ and His light has helped you find an answer to a question you've had or feel peace recently.

Sometimes the light appears faint, but as we take steps forward in faith, our understanding will increase, and the light will grow brighter. And Christ will be with us through it all, illuminating our path.

NOV 18–24: "THAT EVIL MAY BE DONE AWAY"

ETHER 6–11

Ether 6:12

And they did land upon the shore of the promised land. And when they had set their feet upon the shores of the promised land they bowed themselves down upon the face of the land, and did humble themselves before the Lord, and did shed tears of joy before the Lord, because of the multitude of his tender mercies over them.

TALKING POINT

As you study Ether 6–11 this week, consider using a study journal and/or marking your scriptures. Try to turn each real-life story into a personal-life metaphor. Write down the lessons you learn from each metaphor you find.

The very first class I officially registered for in college was poetry. In that class, I learned about the beauty and power of a good metaphor. The scriptures can often be read metaphorically to unlock deeper meanings and applications. Trying to see real-life scriptural events as metaphors of eternal truths is part of what Nephi meant when he told us to "liken all scriptures unto us, that it might be for our profit and learning" (1 Nephi 19:23).

In Ether 6, for example, the Jaredites travel in their unique barges across a treacherous ocean. Assisted by God, they arrive at the promised land. When we read Ether 6:4–12 as a metaphor for our mortal journeys on earth, the verses burst with hope-filled truths about heaven's continual assistance and God's tender mercies that sustain us in times of darkness.

In Ether 6, we also read about stones that God made into lights so that the Jaredites could see in their dark ships (see verses 2–3). What might those stones represent in our own lives as we cross "the great waters" of mortality? Just as "[Jesus] used . . . metaphors to make a deeper impression upon the minds of the children of men"

(Wilford Woodruff, in *Journal of Discourses*, 2:194), we can each try
to see beyond the literal stories in the scriptures and turn them into
application-packed personal metaphors.

_____

_____

_____

_____

_____

_____

_____

_____

_____

_____

_____

_____

_____

_____

_____

_____

_____

_____

_____

_____

_____

_____

_____

_____

_____

_____

_____

NOV 25–DEC 1: "BY FAITH ALL THINGS ARE FULFILLED"

ETHER 12–15

Ether 12:6

And now, I, Moroni, would speak somewhat concerning these things; I would show unto the world that faith is things which are hoped for and not seen; wherefore, dispute not because ye see not, for ye receive no witness until after the trial of your faith.

Sometimes in the Church we hear "I know the Church is true" and believe that we must arrive at a place of absolute knowledge in order to have a solid testimony. But conversion is much more of a daily process than an exact destination. There is no final testimony tent to camp out at until Jesus comes again. Let's reframe our understanding of what it takes to be converted.

Although we don't need to worry about making it to one specific, perfect point in our path of conversion, we can't expect to be truly converted without consistently working for it. We can't just go to the gym one time and expect to be strong. If we're going to progress and prosper spiritually, we need to strengthen our faith muscles daily.

Speaking of Moroni's words in Ether 12:6, Sister Bonnie L. Oscarson shared, "In our world where instant gratification is the expectation, we are often guilty of expecting the reward without having to work for it. I believe Moroni is telling us that we must do the work first and exercise faith by living the gospel, and then we will receive the witness that it is true. True conversion occurs as you continue to act upon the doctrines you know are true and keep the commandments, day after day, month after month" ("Be Ye Converted," *Ensign* or *Liahona*, November 2013).

It takes work, but consistently striving to receive, strengthen, and keep our testimonies is worth every effort. And the "witness . . . after the trial of your faith" will be more wonderful than you can imagine (Ether 12:6).

TALKING POINT

What habits have you created that help you feed your faith on a daily basis? Choose one to focus on this week, then write down how working on this habit helped strengthen your testimony.

DEC 2–8: "TO KEEP THEM IN THE RIGHT WAY"

MORONI 1–6

Moroni 6:8

But as oft as they repented and sought forgiveness, with real intent, they were forgiven.

The process of becoming like God can be a bumpy one. Fortunately for us, the atoning sacrifice of Jesus Christ "encircles [us] in the arms of safety" (Alma 34:16), allowing us to learn from our mistakes without being condemned by them. The prophet Moroni taught that the only way we can ever succeed in becoming like God is by "relying alone upon the merits of Christ, who was the author and the finisher of [our] faith" (Moroni 6:4).

President Dieter F. Uchtdorf said that Heavenly Father's primary purpose is "to mentor us, exalt us, and lead us to His fulness" ("Perfect Love Casteth Out Fear," *Ensign* or *Liahona*, May 2017). And so it is with His perfect Son, Jesus Christ. I love the idea of Jesus being our mentor, personally demonstrating and assisting in our quest for godliness, helping us learn and heal from our sins.

We certainly won't become whole and complete like God in this life. The plan of redemption was based on the reality that we would all fall painfully short in this life, hence the need for a Savior. Our job in this life is to keep striving and retain "a determination to serve him to the end" (Moroni 6:3). Remember what we collectively express in the sacrament prayers each week: "that [we] are *willing* to take upon [us] the name of thy Son" (Moroni 4:3; emphasis added). As long as we are *willing* to keep *striving* to be like God each day, the time will come where "when he shall appear we shall be like him" (Moroni 7:48).

TALKING POINT

Elder Dieter F. Uchtdorf said that "sins are opportunities for greater self-awareness, deeper and more honest love for others, and refinement through repentance. . . .
. . . They are part of our progress" ("God among Us," *Liahona*, May 2021). Start a journal entry this week about how you've grown into a more godly person through what you've learned from your sins.

Supplemental Study Content
Scan the QR code to access President Russell M. Nelson's talk "Perfection Pending."

DEC 9–15: "MAY CHRIST LIFT THEE UP"

MORONI 7–9

Moroni 7:16

For behold, the Spirit of Christ is given to every man, that he may know good from evil; wherefore, I show unto you the way to judge; for every thing which inviteth to do good, and to persuade to believe in Christ, is sent forth by the power and gift of Christ; wherefore ye may know with a perfect knowledge it is of God.

Have you ever hesitated to act on a prompting because you didn't know whether or not it was actually a prompting? This is something many have dealt with. It may feel like wandering around without a GPS. God is asking us to act on the best information we have at the time, learning to trust in His voice and, in the process, grow in godly confidence.

Sister Michelle D. Craig taught, "Our souls long for a connection with our heavenly home. We want to feel needed and useful. But at times we struggle to distinguish between our own thoughts and the gentle impressions of the Spirit. Prophets, ancient and modern, have taught that if something 'invites and entices to do good, it comes from Christ'" ("Spiritual Capacity," *Ensign* or *Liahona*, November 2019).

When we have a thought or prompting to do anything good, it is from God. Give Him the credit. Don't get confused or stuck with the "is it me or is it God" debate—just act on the impression. Even if it was your idea, you are letting God know that you want to have Him talk to you and you are willing to take action.

Sometimes we don't see the providential hand of heaven until

> **TALKING POINT**
>
> For one week, try and act quickly on any prompting or good impression you receive. Give God the credit and see what miracles happen when you are willing to let Him use you for His purposes.

hindsight sets in. But then we can look back and realize how God was orchestrating the perfect miracle for both us and those we served.

DEC 16–22: "COME UNTO CHRIST, AND BE PERFECTED IN HIM"

MORONI 10

Moroni 10:4, 29

And when ye shall receive these things, I would exhort you that ye would ask God, the Eternal Father, in the name of Christ, if these things are not true; and if ye shall ask with a sincere heart, with real intent, having faith in Christ, he will manifest the truth of it unto you, by the power of the Holy Ghost.

And God shall show unto you, that that which I have written is true.

I was eighteen years old when I received an undeniable witness from God that the Book of Mormon is true and divine in its origins. That witness transformed me into a new person. I only regret that I waited so long to finally take the Book of Mormon challenge.

In his final words, Moroni invites everyone who reads the Book of Mormon to "ask God, the Eternal Father, in the name of Christ, if these things are not true." He then promises, "If ye shall ask with a sincere heart, with real intent, having faith in Christ, he will manifest the truth of it unto you, by the power of the Holy Ghost" (Moroni 10:4).

My witness from God came after I had fulfilled my personal commitment to read every word on the 531 pages of the Book of Mormon. I even read the words "THE END" written at the bottom of the last page! My witness of the Book of Mormon's divinity was accompanied by a sure witness of God's reality, of the unfailing love of Jesus Christ, and of Joseph Smith's prophetic calling.

I can personally witness that if you read the Book of Mormon with a humble, open heart, God will reveal to you through His Holy Spirit that He is the source of the book. With that spiritual witness, you will come to know many additional liberating truths about God and His plan. As Moroni put it, "By the power of the Holy Ghost ye may know the truth of *all* things" (Moroni 10:5; emphasis added).

TALKING POINT

Have you received an undeniable witness that the Book of Mormon is of God? If so, look for an opportunity to share your witness with someone this week, and consider how you can further strengthen your current testimony. If you have not yet received a divine witness, don't panic. Prayerfully read and contemplate the Book of Mormon challenge, found in Moroni 10:3–7. Pay close attention to the thoughts and feelings the Spirit gives you as you read and study this week, then act in faith— ask God for a witness from the Holy Ghost! Record your impressions.

DEC 23–29: "HE SHALL COME INTO THE WORLD TO REDEEM HIS PEOPLE"

CHRISTMAS

Christmas through the Book of Mormon

Christmas carols can transport us beyond time and culture. Their hope-filled messages are timeless and beautiful. These are the words to one of my favorite Christmas hymns:

> Joy to the world, the Lord is come;
> Let earth receive her King!
> Let ev'ry heart prepare him room,
> And Saints and angels sing,
> And Saints and angels sing,
> And Saints, and Saints and angels sing.
> ("Joy to the World," *Hymns*, no. 201)

TALKING POINT

Compare the Christmas story in Luke 2 with what we learn about Christ's birth from the Book of Mormon. Scan the QR code for a list of scripture references that can help you with this activity.
Have a Merry Christmas!

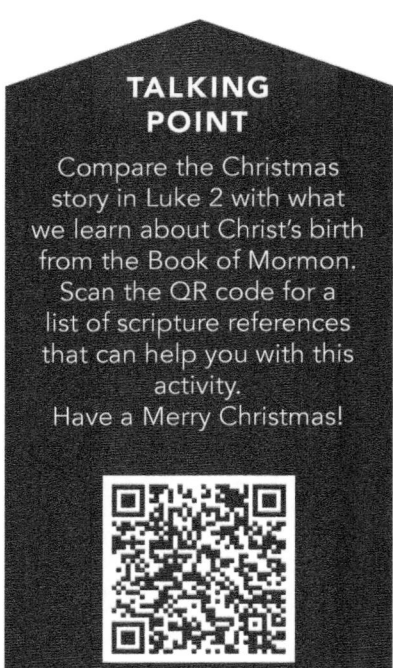

It is a blessing to see the Christmas story through the lenses of the Old and New Testament. Through the Restoration, we are also blessed to have the Book of Mormon perspective. The Book of Mormon is the record of people from another time who were invited to prepare for, anticipate, and then receive their King. They went through cycles of struggle and prosperity. Some turned to God and waited for His coming while others did not.

What have you learned from the Book of Mormon this year that can prepare your heart to receive the Savior like "Joy to the World" says? What have the people and the stories from this incredible book of scripture taught you about Him?

ABOUT GANEL-LYN CONDIE

GANEL-LYN CONDIE IS A POPULAR motivational speaker known for inspiring others with her unique honesty, authenticity, and spirit. She is dedicated to her family, faith, and inspiring everyone around her. She loves teaching others with speaking and writing. She graduated summa cum laude from Arizona State University with a bachelor's in education and a minor in psychology.

Ganel-Lyn has experienced healing from a major chronic illness and is the mother to two miracle children. After the heart-breaking suicide of her forty-year-old sister, Ganel-Lyn is constantly working toward prevention for others. She lives with an open heart and feels passionate about sharing principles that will empower others to live life with more joy. She is a regular television/radio guest and hosted the popular show *Talk of Him* and still hosts *The Middle*.

Ganel-Lyn's talks and books have encouraged thousands of people all over the world. She loves growing older with her supportive husband, Rob, and aims to keep learning and loving.

ABOUT JOHN FOSSUM

JOHN FOSSUM ORIGINALLY PLANNED TO teach college literature courses for his vocation, but life unexpectedly led him to a career in the Church Education System. He has taught in a variety of contexts throughout his time as a religious educator, including institute classes for young single adults and religion classes for adults, though he currently teaches seminary full-time. John also cohosted the popular show *Talk of Him*. He is married to Sarah Packer, whom he credits for many of his deepest insights into the gospel. They live in Pleasant Grove, Utah, and have five children. John loves to travel with his wife, and he enjoys eating anything chocolate.